# Stitching and Stuffing

# Stitching

Illustrated by Judy Francis

Preface and Two Original Designs by Jerry Kott

# and Stuffing

## The New Needlecraft of Soft Sculpture

### Karen Levine

Rawson Associates Publishers, Inc.    New York

COLOR PLATES by Stephen T. Anderson

Library of Congress Cataloging in Publication Data

Levine, Karen.
  Stitching and stuffing.
  Includes index.
  1.  Textile crafts.  2.  Soft sculpture.  I.  Title.
TT669.L48    746.4    76–53671
ISBN 0–89256–020–7

*For Fanny Weingrod, my grandmother,*
*and*
*Alan Gelb, my husband,*
*with gratitude and with love*

# *Acknowledgments*

There are several people who helped me, in different ways, to write STITCHING AND STUFFING. I thank my parents for always taking seriously my interests in crafts and in writing, and indulging my creative needs—both physically and spiritually.

Thank you, Judy Francis, for your absolute professionalism, not just in providing beautiful illustrations, but in allowing a dialogue, allowing my input, and always having everything on schedule.

Thanks to Jerry Kott for trusting me enough to share his talent and his valuable time.

Thanks to Evelyn O'Connor for all the special care she's given to STITCHING AND STUFFING and for making it as beautiful a book as it is.

And I thank Sandi Gelles-Cole for excelling in every way as both a friend and an editor. It mattered.

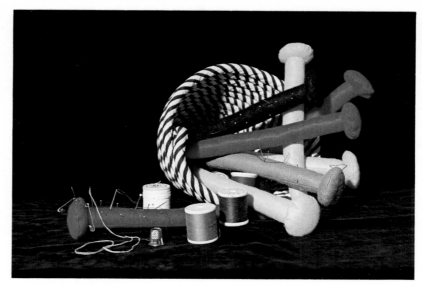

*Pin Pincushion, page 31*

*Sculpted Face Vase, page 94*

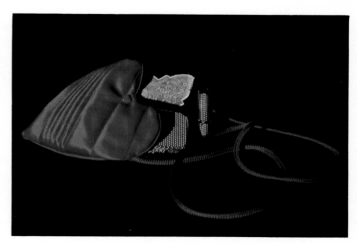

*Heart Evening Bag, page 77*

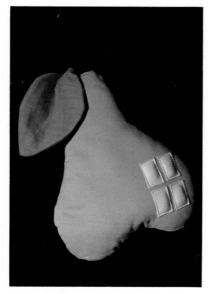

*Pear Pillow, page 35*

*Name Mobile, page 41*

*Coil Pot, page 89*

*Face Belt, page 63*

*Auto Mirror, page 54*

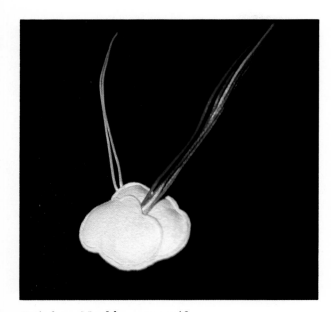

*Rainbow Necklace, page 49*

*Fern Pillow, page 69*

# Preface by Jerry Kott

For the purpose of this book "soft sculpture" can be loosely defined as fabric manipulation. It's a very broad definition, to be sure, but it's a very broad field as well, limited only by the word "soft" and your imagination. As you work your way into our book, you'll get some sense of the scope of the medium. You can approach it from lots of angles, making purely decorative objects or making things that are more practical. The line between the practical and the decorative becomes very thin, however, since our objective, and motivation, is to combine the two. Surely an evening bag or a pincushion should be as attractive as it is useful. In fact, everything we use *should* be as beautifully designed as its function allows. Why not?

Although art critics didn't acknowledge soft sculpture as a fine-arts form until the mid-1960s, people have been stuffing and stitching for as long as they've had fabric and thread. We'd be hard put to trace the appearance of the first pillow, but expressions in the "soft" medium that are considerably more complicated than a pillow—rag dolls, beanbags, Christmas-tree decorations—are certainly a part of American folk-art history. All of these things were made by people with little more to guide them than their eyes and their imagination. These people were not the prominent artists of their day. They were not dependent on the sale of their product for a living. They were simply using their hands to make their houses prettier, their children happier, and their winters pass more quickly. The dolls that they made may not have looked much like "Tiny Tears" or "Chatty Patty," but their eccentricity was part of their charm.

Ultimately, we would like you to feel comfortable enough with cutting and creating patterns to move out on your own and develop a unique style. All of the projects outlined in this book will provide you with take-off points, from which you can personalize your creation. Even when you follow the pattern exactly, it is your approach—your choice of material, your variation of size or stitching—that will make the piece yours. Keep in mind that the same design made in two different fabrics, or stuffed with two different materials, can evoke entirely different feelings.

Another important thing to keep in mind is that soft sculpture is fun. Almost always, there is a bit of whimsy. Even when we look at the medium as it appears in museums, we can't help but laugh at Claes Oldenberg's huge ice bag. It's funny because it is reality distorted, and it strikes a familiar chord of inspiration. Most of us, at one point or another, have had a headache that might have inspired just such a sculpture.

Always, the creator is playing with the observer's eye. Think of something very hard, or perhaps very sharp, and play with the concept of opposites. Perhaps you might try to design a set of stuffed hanging knives as a kitchen decoration. Play with the concept of the unexpected—on its most banal level, remember the gun shooting a flag that says BANG. On a more artistic level, imagine an oversized satin plant set smack in the middle of a shelf filled with the real thing. Why not make a pincushion in the shape of a big pin? Look around you now and pay some attention to the texture of your surroundings. Texture is something we tend to take for granted, and the things we take most for granted are the things that deserve most to be played with. Their manipulation carries the promise of surprise, and in the medium of soft sculpture such surprise can be very entertaining. By the time you've finished making the projects in this book you will be ready to "soften up" your own environment.

Remember that it pays to think practically as well as whimsically. A black satin evening bag in the shape of a swan that has no room for a comb makes no sense, so our design for the evening bag includes all of the pragmatic details. While "soft" jewelry must work as a soft sculpture, it must also work as a piece of jewelry. It must fasten securely, and fit comfortably around your wrist or neck. A baby's doll must be washable and strong if we want a baby to enjoy it. An adult's doll (yes, there *are* dolls for adults) doesn't have to meet the same requirements.

Hopefully, I've touched on enough in this preface to excite you about the possibilities of soft sculpture, and to assure you that there is no limit to what you'll be able to do with some newly acquired skills and a great deal of imagination. But my enthusiasm comes from my experience, and your enthusiasm is bound to grow as you move through the book.

—JERRY KOTT

*New York City*
*January 1977*

# Contents

# The Stuff of
# Soft Sculpture

# Why Stitch and Stuff?

Not too long ago I was called for jury duty. Much of jury duty, I discovered, involves sitting in a large room with other prospective jurors and waiting to be called. If you are called to be interviewed for a jury, and are rejected (as I was), you go back to the big jurors' waiting room. After a few days of waiting, I decided to buy some wool and begin a sweater for a forthcoming niece or nephew, due four months later. It would be the first baby on my husband's side of the family, so the event was anticipated with a great deal of excitement. I began work. The wool was bright orange, and the baby seemed more and more a reality as the sweater took shape.

At some point, the rather pugnacious-looking lady sitting on my left leaned over and said, "It's cheaper to buy." The message given, she turned back to her newspaper. I was a bit surprised, but explained that it was the first baby and she could surely understand my enthusiasm. I continued to knit, and she continued to read, as though we had never had the exchange. A few minutes later she leaned toward me again and said, quite adamantly, "It's cheaper and it's better to buy." I wasn't looking for a fight. I didn't particularly want to be where I was, and would have been grateful to be left alone. But her voice had developed a surly tone, as if there were some greater principle she was defending—free enterprise, perhaps, or something else equally holy. I explained my motivation in greater detail, acknowledging that while it might well be cheaper to buy a baby sweater than to make one, and that store-bought baby sweaters could be of the very finest quality, I was having fun seeing the tiny sweater take shape. I was having fun, and my pleasure was adequate compensation for the cost. A woman sitting in front of us turned around to defend my position. "Just think how good she'll feel when the baby wears that sweater," she offered. I nodded, grateful for the support. The curmudgeonly lady turned back to her paper, and for a while I continued to work on my sweater. There was silence.

Finally, after five minutes or so, she turned to me again and put her face very close to mine. "You gotta be a jerk to make it yourself," she sputtered. And she gathered up her vinyl shopping bag and walked away.

I doubt that the shopping-bag lady is reading this book right now. But you are, so surely you understand why I chose to make, rather than buy, the orange baby sweater. People who make things don't need any justification for what they're doing. We make things because the process and the results give us great pleasure. Before I begin to discuss my specific involvement with soft sculpture, I'd like to talk a bit about the implications of enjoying crafts, and about my own experience. My past experience and the feelings that motivate me to make things are probably not all that different from your own.

When I was somewhere between the ages of five and ten, my grandmother taught me how to make an apron. Although I didn't like the actual making of the apron very much, I loved having an apron that I had made. When I finished the first, I embarked on a wardrobe of aprons, experimenting with differently shaped pockets, with full aprons and half aprons, and with every variety of trimming. My grandmother had designed millinery, and had all sorts of feathers and shiny buttons. Whatever she had showed up on my aprons.

When she was convinced that I was serious,

my grandmother bought me a miniature, hand-operated Singer sewing machine, and both my output and my production time doubled. Each time I finished an apron I felt the same sense of satisfaction. Each time I saw someone wearing one of my aprons I felt an even greater sense of satisfaction. If the lady sitting next to me at jury duty had ever felt that particular kind of pride, she wouldn't have argued cost and quality with me.

My grandmother, of course, had a much more diverse repertoire than I. She made virtually everything: curtains, dresses, bedspreads, hats. It simply never occurred to her that there might be something in fabric that she couldn't make. She somehow left that attitude—with a multitude of variations—with me, and despite the fact that it's gotten me into a great deal of trouble (for example, the couch I began building that a professional upholsterer had to finish), I'm tremendously grateful to her for my inheritance.

As I mentioned, there was a bit of variation between my grandmother's interest in making things and mine. She was interested primarily in sewing, and over the years my enthusiasm for crafts became much more general. Shortly after my grandmother taught me to sew, my mother taught me to knit. A few years later my father taught me about woodworking. In college I studied pottery. After graduating, I took courses in silversmithing. But though the crafts varied, the attitude that motivated me remained constant, as did the pleasure I derived from the process and results of my efforts. I never like to feel that I have nothing to do, and somehow all the projects I have going eventually get completed. I just finished a needlepoint I started three years ago.

It's very difficult to talk to a "nonmaker" about the satisfaction and total involvement I feel from my crafts. Some of my closest friends—although considerably more refined than the angry juror—echo her sentiments. They like what I make for them, but harbor the suspicion that I'm just a bit off center. Which brings me to soft sculpture.

On Christmas Day, 1975, my husband and I went to a very small afternoon party. It was a quiet gathering of about eight people, one of whom was sleeping in a chair. Our host explained that the sleeping man was Jerry Kott, a friend of theirs who was a "soft sculptor" and had been up all night filling an order.

A few days earlier I had found a bag full of felt squares sitting on a shelf in my closet. I think they were once intended for a big wall hanging . . . that never materialized. For some unaccountable reason, I cut the felt and made a soft car, with people hanging out a window. As I said, I don't know what compelled me to make the car, other than the fact that I had the fabric and was in the mood to do something with it. When Jerry woke up we began to talk about soft sculpture, about Claes Oldenberg, and especially about Jerry's work and my own little car.

Jerry had been stitching and stuffing fabric for several years, and the designs he described to me sounded very exciting. He suggested that I come down to his loft sometime and check out his setup. By the time the party was over, we had made an appointment.

As you've probably gathered, I tend to approach my crafts with a great deal of enthusiasm. After I visited Jerry and saw his work, I could not think of very much else besides soft sculpture. We talked for a long time about the potential of shaping fabrics. Jerry showed me different experiments of his—some of which had worked, some of which hadn't—and encouraged me to test my own ideas. He was terrifically generous in his support, and already at the point of reaping the rewards from the gamble he took on his own talent. I went home and made more stuffed things.

The more I made, the more I enjoyed soft sculpture. Jerry and I met regularly and discussed our work and the nature of the craft. Soft sculpture appealed particularly to my sense of whimsy and humor, as I hope it will appeal to yours. Also appealing is the idea of beginning and completing an interesting project in one sitting. Several of the projects included in this book can be done in a relatively short time.

I hope that your enjoyment of soft sculpture grows with your experience, as mine did, and that you find stitching and stuffing fabric an exciting means of expression.

# How to Use This Book

*Stitching and Stuffing* is a very carefully and thoughtfully designed book, with many special features. All of these features were designed with your learning experience in mind. Everything that Jerry, my editor, and I could think of to make a concept or technique more accessible is included. But you have to know how to use the book in order to take advantage of our brain-storming. So let's take it from the very beginning.

## FABRIC AND STUFFING CHAPTERS

Before you even begin to make the first project, you should read the chapters on fabric and stuffing. As I point out in these chapters, it's important for a craftsperson to understand her media, and the cram course we offer in these pages—although only the tip of the iceberg—is enough to get you going. But our information on fabrics and stuffings will do much more than prepare you for the projects in this book. It should serve as a frequent source of reference in all of your dealings with fabric. I'm confident that you will go on from here to make other soft sculptures, in which case you will undoubtedly use these chapters to check for potential problems in fabric compatibility, cleanability, and durability. Even if you are thinking about sewing a dress, picking a fabric for curtains, or re-stuffing an old chair, these two chapters should be the first place you go for information.

## GRADUATED PROJECTS

When you have read about fabrics and stuffings, you are ready to begin soft sculpting, and it's important that as a beginner, you begin at the beginning—with the soft-pin pincushion. The ten projects I've offered are arranged in very specific order, and should be tackled in exactly their order of presentation. Most obvious is the fact that each project is a bit more difficult than the one before. But the projects progress in other ways as well. Often a specific skill you learn in one project is applied in a later project. Although I explain each step of every project in great detail, the first time a new skill is presented I offer it in its least complicated form. If you have the experience of an uncomplicated application, the complicated version is always less intimidating. Look at the picture of the face belt, and then look at the photograph of the face vase. The vase is considerably more detailed and sculpted than the belt, but some of the techniques involved in making each of them are similar. The belt is a first step toward the vase.

So be patient with each project. By the time you reach the last, there will be a great number of things you do automatically that seemed terribly difficult when you began.

## THE ILLUSTRATIONS

The illustrations for *Stitching and Stuffing* were drawn by Judy Francis, who has a remarkable talent for turning my semi-intelligible babbling into clean, clear line drawings. Always refer to the illustrations, and when you need to, refer back to them. On several of the more difficult projects we have arranged the text so that it appears directly below that step of a project which it details. I suggest that in *all* cases you read through the entire project before you actually begin to make it, but in these specially coordinated projects the initial read-through is even more important. It's always easier to get somewhere if you know where you're going.

Often I'll suggest that you look at an illustration for an earlier project to clarify what you're doing on another. Since many of the techniques you use in later projects are explained in earlier ones, if you check back to a previous illustration the whole process will probably click a lot faster.

## THE TRACING PAGES

The tracing pages, a very special feature of this book, do away with a great number of complications. With very few exceptions, every time you have a project that involves a tracing page the same procedure for using it is applied. Detailed instructions are given throughout the book, but basically you will be tracing the pattern onto a sheet of ordinary typing paper and then transferring it, by means of carbon paper, to cardboard or oak tag. (See illustration 1.) Cardboard patterns insure greater accuracy than paper patterns, since paper can slip.

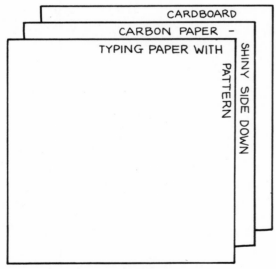

*Illustration 1*

Two of the exceptions to the above process are the face belt and the face vase. With these two projects the design is traced onto regular typing paper, which is then pinned directly to the fabric. A piece of seamstress tracing paper is then inserted between the paper pattern and the fabric, and the detailed design is retraced with a ballpoint pen directly onto the fabric. (See illustration 2.) This process is really very much the same as the earlier process, but differs in materials.

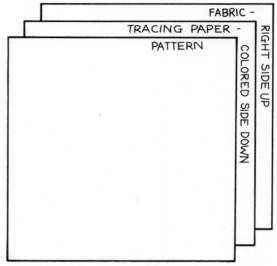

*Illustration 2*

(There are several different kinds of seamstress tracing paper, and it doesn't make much difference which one you use. I use Scovill Dritz Tracing Paper, because it's what the store nearest my home carries. If no one in your area has what you want, I suggest you write to: Sewing Notions Division, Scovill Manufacturing Company, Department 552X, Spartanburg, South Carolina 29301, and inquire about buying the paper directly from them. But I'd be very surprised if you had to resort to the manufacturer for this item.)

If you look carefully at each tracing page, you'll notice that the beginning lines of a grid trim the perimeter of each page. This feature is designed to encourage and simplify your own experimentation. The tracer designs are written to be made exactly to size, as they appear. But you may decide that you'd like to see the same project three times the size I suggest. To turn any tracing design into a grid design, you need only connect the lines we've begun, and once you have a grid there's no limit to how large or small you can make an object.

## THE GRIDS

Grids are a way of simplifying the reproduction of designs. Billboard painters use them to transfer small paintings to the huge billboards that clutter our highways. The theory behind a grid is simply that it's easier to reproduce a small detail than it is to look at an entire picture. The theory works beautifully, and is lots of fun to play with. Go through a magazine until you find a sketch that appeals to you. If you draw a grid over it, and a larger grid on a clean piece of paper, you'll find that you can reproduce the original sketch—even if you have no talent at drawing.

There is only one project in this book that is specifically a grid project. On the pear pillow you are given instructions on how big to make your pattern if you want your pillow to be the same size as mine. Construct a grid in which each square is 1¼″ wide. Then connect the lines on the rim of the tracing page to form a grid. Simply reproduce the pattern, line by line, square by square, to correspond with the grid in the book. (See illustration 3.)

The technique of using a grid offers you tremendous range. You can reproduce virtually anything. I've already suggested experimenting with the reproduction of magazine pictures, but you can use these reproductions in your soft sculpture as well as hang them on the refrigerator door. If you've made the pear pillow and want to make other fruit pillows, you need only find a good picture of a strawberry, banana, or apple in a magazine and draw a grid over it. Once you have drawn the grid, you can transfer the entire design to cardboard. You can make patterns from anything, and with the use of a grid they can all be reduced or enlarged.

I suggest the following formula for enlarging. Begin with a decision as to how large you want your project to be. Measure the length of the picture you will be enlarging, and divide that length into the length you want. The result of this division is the number of times you will be blowing up the original. For example: You find a picture of an apple that measures 4″ in length. You want your apple pillow to measure 16″ in

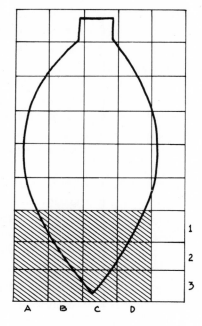

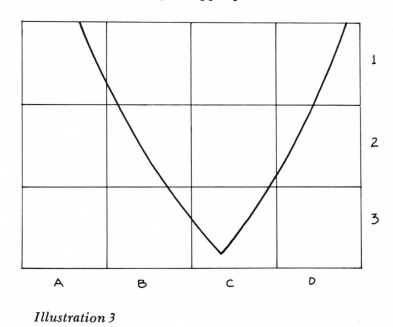

*Illustration 3*

length. Dividing 16 by 4 gives 4, which means that each square on the graph over the original must be enlarged four times. If you drew a 1/4″ graph over the picture, you must now draw a 1″ graph on your oak tag.

It takes some care and patience to reproduce by this method, but the rewards make it well worth your time.

## STITCH GLOSSARY

Although everything in this book can be sewn by hand, my assumption is that you have a sewing machine. Still, sometimes it is best to use a handstitch. Often, these stitches are decorative. When there is an option to use some fancy embroidery stitches, I leave the choice of stitches up to you.

But you will always have to hand-stitch your stuffing hole closed, and do other similar hand finishing. For these instances I have supplied you with four different stitches, plus a special-use decorative stitch. Each is clearly illustrated in the Stitch Glossary.

## PHOTOGRAPHS

Every project in the book has been photographed individually in color, so that you have an idea of where you're going while you're working. Before you begin a project, study the photograph carefully, and keep referring to it while you work.

## SPINOFFS

Although this book appears to be a ten-project workbook, the pages contain suggestions and general instructions for at least three times that many soft sculptures. Ideally, each of the ten projects will serve as a taking-off point. In the introduction to the projects I discuss spinoffs. These spinoffs may alter the original objects by changing their size, shape, or trim; or they may suggest an entirely different project employing some of the techniques you've just learned.

However they vary from the original, make an effort to experiment with the idea of spinning off. This sort of variation is at the heart of soft-sculpture design. I've included some ideas on spinning off to start you thinking originally about design and variation. This kind of thinking is as important to learn as the techniques of stitching and stuffing.

## YOUR OTHER CRAFTS

One of the nicest things about soft sculpture is that it mixes well. It's likely that if you bought this book, you're the kind of person who likes crafts in general and has experimented with other crafts. Use them in your soft sculpture. Most obviously, you can use embroidery skills to decorate fabric sculpture. Or you can apply a needlepoint canvas somewhere on a project.

Some of our projects require quilting. Some lend themselves to macramé. The face belt buckle can certainly be attached to a macramé belt.

But I've seen soft sculpture mixed with pottery, wood, and metal. I've seen pieces of fabric sculpture made from batiked and silk-screened fabrics. You can even hand-paint a piece of fabric before you stuff it.

Keep in mind that soft sculpture is versatile. The "can do" is far greater than the "can't."

# Fabrics

Now that you know something about my background, and something about Jerry, and, of course, something about soft sculpture, it's time for you to learn something about fabric.

Fabric—the stuff from which soft sculpture is made—can be used creatively. But your creative use of the medium is always dependent on your understanding and knowledge of how to use it. Fabrics come in all sorts of finishes, strengths, looks, etc., but unless you know what's available to you, you won't have the vaguest idea of what to apply where. The point of this chapter, really, is to increase your "fabric vocabulary." As you learn about fabric, you'll be better able to think in terms of each fabric's limitations and applications.

It may seem less than crucial to you at first to understand what fabric is, how it's made, and some of the many variations, but trust me on this: The more you know about fabric, the more creative you will be using it.

The most important thing in dealing with any medium of design is for the craftsperson to know some of the most basic characteristics of her materials. A woodworker knows that the decision to use pine, as opposed to using ebony, is not made on purely esthetic grounds. Certain woods lend themselves particularly well to certain purposes. There are questions a woodworker might ask before buying materials: What sort of grain does this wood have? How does the grain affect strength? The questions I ask myself before I choose a fabric serve the same purpose. I once had the unfortunate experience of reupholstering a convertible couch. (Remember when I told you that my self-confidence often caused a great deal of grief?) I went out

and bought a lovely brown fabric, and spent months cutting and laying it over the couch. Finally, after a great deal of pinning and folding, I began to sew. When it was finished, nearly three months after I began, it looked terrific. And it remained terrific-looking for about three weeks. By the end of the third week I noticed that the fabric had begun to wear. After two months there were holes in the seats, and it was time to re-reupholster.

If I had known then what I know now about fabrics, I might not have put so great an effort to waste. I had chosen chenille, a loose-pile fabric, for my reupholstering, not realizing that fabrics like that are simply not constructed to wear well in constant use. So when I suggest that you read this chapter very carefully, and learn the basic questions you should ask yourself when choosing a fabric, my suggestion is based on some very real personal experience!

Some of the basic questions of fabric selection are as follows. Does the fabric come in the right colors/patterns? This question may seem quite natural to you, but as you read on in this chapter you'll realize more and more that fabric design is specific to only certain fabrics. You may want to make a particular piece of sculpture in felt, only to discover that felt is not available in the brightly striped pattern you conjured up.

You must question whether a fabric will hold up well under use. I'm sure that the tragic tale of my upholstering fiasco will stay with you for a while at least. My choice of chenille for my couch made about as much sense as using molded wax for a hot-pot trivet!

Ask yourself, before you buy a fabric, whether

it will clean well; and if you're going to use a washable stuffing, it's a good idea to use a washable fabric. We'll talk more about compatibility between the stuffing and the outer fabric later, but it's worth touching on here. There are stuffings, like polyurethane, that cannot be dry-cleaned. Quite simply, they dissolve when they meet the cleaning fluid. If you were to use an outer fabric that could not be washed—that required dry-cleaning—and stuff it with polyurethane, you would create an uncleanable sculpture. And an uncleanable sculpture makes about as much sense as a lightweight-chenille couch!

You need to ask how flexible a fabric is. Some fabrics present a hard, stiff surface. Satin is one of those fabrics. This sort of surface is neither good nor bad; it is good for certain projects and bad for others. For example, while children often like to touch the satin trim on blankets, they wouldn't be very happy with a satin teddy bear. Satin is smooth and soft unstuffed, but cold and hard stuffed. It should almost never be stuffed very tightly, but then, almost no fabric will look soft if the stuffing is too tightly packed.

These are only a few of the questions you will learn to ask, and you can answer them all with the minimal information in this chapter.

## DIGGING IN

Do you remember Rumpelstiltskin? As I recall, he was found out while in a frenzy of spinning flax into gold. Trust me on this: No one has ever spun flax into gold. But spinning, the conversion of a raw substance into fibers and thread, is at the root of fabric making. All woven fabrics are composed of fibers that are made into thread. Fibers can be classified into two categories: natural and man-made. The natural fibers are: *silk,* spun by little worms in their cocoons; *cotton,* which was once the main industry of the South; *wool,* sheared off the back of sheep; and *flax,* the plant from which linen is made. Natural fibers are, simply, fibers we get from nature.

In contrast to the fibers we find in nature are the man-made, or synthetic, fibers. These fibers do not exist as fibers in their natural state. They must be transformed into fibers through some chemical process. They might begin as liquids in big vats, or as small marbles, from which a thin thread is extracted, or even as glass. We all know that the synthetics, with names like dacron, rayon (the first man-made fabric), nylon, acetate, Banlon, etc., have revolutionized the fabric industry. If you ever visit New York, I urge you to visit the Burlington Mill. It's a fantastic free exhibit in which nearly every fabric-making process is demonstrated.

But enough of fibers. Let's move on to the threads, and what can be done with them to make fabric. Basically, there are three ways of turning threads into fabric: They can be woven; they can be compressed; or they can be knitted. The three processes are very different from one another, and produce fabrics that serve very different needs. Within each category there are fabrics that you will use for soft sculpture. But the important thing to know, as I said earlier, is what to use when, and why.

Let's begin with weaving. Take a look at your screen door. It's a fairly good representation of what a basic woven fabric would look like if you put it under a powerful microscope. Basically, there are horizontal threads and vertical threads that are interlocked, over and under. If you've ever looped a potholder, you know the process. The vertical yarns are called the warp, and they're always the same. Variations in weave are a result of how the horizontal yarn is looped around the warp. Remember your screen door. It represents the most basic of all weaves; this simple interlocking of thread is called the *tabby* weave. The horizontal and vertical threads are connected with a simple under-and-over weave. This type of connection provides a very dense and strong fabric—like most of the brightly colored cottons.

The other weaves that you're familiar with are probably the *twill* and, of course, the *satin* weaves. In a twill, the horizontal thread crosses over two warps for each one it goes under, and in the satin the thread passes over four or more warps. Think about satin for a minute. It's shiny and smooth, it catches very easily, and it's not very strong. All of these characteristics are a direct result of the weave. Since the thread passes over so many more warps than it passes under, it becomes almost like a big, big, basting stitch. But let's save the specific information of fabrics for later. The important thing for you to understand now is what a weave is, and a basic weave is as simple as a tic-tac-toe board.

The most important tangent to your understanding of weave and how it relates to soft sculpture is the concept of the *bias*. If you take any woven fabric and pull it along either the vertical (warp) or the horizontal threads, you'll notice that it doesn't have much give. If we're going to stuff fabrics, elasticity is obviously very important. The best way to achieve elasticity in a woven fabric is to turn it around slightly so that you're pulling on the diagonal. Now think back to tic-tac-toe, and picture this: You have just won a game by making three X's, one in the center, one in the upper right corner, and one in the lower left corner. You draw a line through the squares. That line represents the bias of a fabric. Experiment by pulling on a piece of fabric in different directions. (Look at illustration 4.) As a rule, unless otherwise indicated, when you cut a woven fabric for a soft sculpture, try to cut on the bias.

The next main group of fabrics, after the woven ones, are the knits. If you looked at a knit under a microscope, it would look nothing like your screen door. Those of you who have ever made a sweater know that the threads in a knit are *looped* together, rather than woven. This looping procedure, as a rule, gives great elasticity and flexibility, and the techniques for looping have as many variations as the techniques for weaving. In recent years the knitting process has been mechanized, and we've been offered a much larger variety of knits. There are single knits, which you see in the average sweater; bonded knits, with a layer of bonding

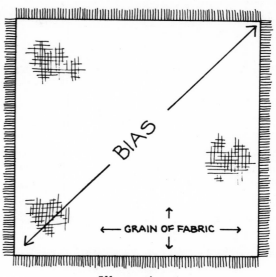

*Illustration 4*

on one side which gives strength but less elasticity; and, of course, double knits. Double knits are the most important for soft sculpture. They are actually two layers of knitted fabric joined together.

All knits come in a vast variety of colors, patterns, and textures.

The final classification of fabric construction is the nonwovens. These fabrics are made by taking loose fibers and compressing them under heat and steam. Chief among this sort of fabric is felt. Compressed fabrics are easily identified. They look, under the magnifying glass, like Kleenex, and, just like Kleenex, if you pull at them hard enough, they come apart. As I said, we will use felt more than any other compressed fabric, but the iron-on interfacing used in many of the projects of this book is also a compressed fabric.

The rest of what you need to know about fabrics is very specific. You will no doubt find that the rest of this chapter will serve as a good reference for as long as you're making soft sculpture. Whenever you plan a project, check the fabric here first. Then check the next chapter for the best stuffing, and make certain to coordinate the two. This sort of simple research is your guarantee against disappointment!

## THE WOVEN FABRICS

### Cotton

We all know what cotton is. It's that fabric that we either can't find shirts made of, or can't afford when we do! It's the most popular of fabrics, and easily obtained from a fabric store. It comes in a wide variety of colors and patterns, and ranges in texture from muslin (an unbleached, tightly woven cotton) to canvas (a coarse, colorful, more durable material.) "Cotton" is available in lots of the weaves of fabrics with which you're familiar. Denim is a kind of cotton. Corduroy can be made from cotton. You needn't memorize a list of all cotton fabrics, though. Just ask the salesperson in your fabric store about the composition of the goods that interest you. Often—and this is where the trouble comes in for me when I shop for a shirt—cotton is combined with synthetic fibers. In many instances the combination increases the practical applications of the fabric, making it shrink less, fade less, or require no ironing. I still like shirts to be 100 percent cotton, but the combination fabrics work very well for soft sculpture.

*Characteristics.* Cotton, as I've said, comes in a great variety of textures and weights, ranging anywhere from a very fine voile to canvas. The texture of the fabric depends on the quality of yarn used in the weaving. Just as the different weights of fabric look different, they also feel different. Generally, the feel of cotton is not anything extraordinary. It isn't slippery, or flashy, or plush. Unlike satin, cotton doesn't feel luxurious. Rather, it has a very natural homespun feel, and a hard, easily creased finish.

*Workability.* As a rule, cotton is very easy to work with. It stays flat during cutting, and doesn't require a great deal of pinning. Also, in all but the coarsest cottons, the edges don't unravel when you cut. In the coarser grains, it's usually a good idea to cut with pinking shears to

avoid unraveling, and it's always a good idea to handle your cut fabric as little as possible. If you don't have pinking shears, and want to cut a piece of canvas or some other very loosely woven, rough cotton, I'd suggest that you sew a row of stay stitching along the edge you have cut.

*Sewing.* Cotton is the easiest of almost any fabric to sew. It doesn't bunch up and gather, and even with minimal pinning it won't slide.

*Durability.* The strength of cotton is determined by the quality and texture of the yarn used to construct the fabric. As a rule, cotton is strong when it's combined with synthetic fibers. Cotton is much better than the synthetics when it comes to static buildup. This static-free quality is a big plus when it comes to workability. Always check 100-percent cotton for colorfastness and for shrinkage by testing a small sample of the fabric you're using.

*Cleaning.* Generally, cotton can be machine-washed if you allow for shrinkage. I recommend using cold-water wash for bright colors and for any cotton/synthetic combination. If you're at all nervous about washing cotton, however, you can always have it dry-cleaned.

*In general.* Cotton has very few limitations, other than the ones you put on it. It is almost always a good choice of fabric for the beginner, since it's widely available, washable, and easy to use.

### Satin

I've never slept on satin sheets, but I've never slept on a waterbed, either. Both of them are things I'd like to try. Satin is associated with luxury, for many good reasons. First of all, non-synthetic satin is very expensive. Before the synthetics were developed, few people could afford the luxury of the slippery fabric. Today satin is available at reasonable prices in various synthetics, all of which I recommend.

*Characteristics.* Let me repeat, just for the sake of form, that satin is a smooth, slippery, lustrous fabric. Earlier in this chapter I explained how the weave of satin is responsible for its appearance, so I needn't go back to all that technical data. What you need to remember about satin is that while it feels smooth to the touch, it's not really a *soft* fabric. In fact, satin's smooth finish makes it a hard fabric. It has an expensive look to it and comes in a wide variety of rich and flashy colors. And, as Jerry Kott says, "A little flash never hurt anyone!"

*Workability*. Satin is easy to cut and gives a good, crisp edge. But beware. With even a minimum of handling, that crisp edge will begin to fray. There's not much you can do to avoid the fraying edges of satin, other than to be prepared with everything you're going to do, and do it smoothly. An important precaution is to *not* pull the fraying threads. If you pull, it will only fray more.

Also, because satin is slippery, when you lay it with the right sides together (which is generally the way to lay fabric) it will tend to slide unless adequately pinned. There is none of the natural friction you have with cotton or a velour. Pinning satin can be a problem. Again, because of the nature of the weave, pins can leave holes. Make an effort to use special satin pins, rather than ordinary seamstress pins. Satin pins are longer and thinner, thereby enabling you to take more fabric with each pin and use fewer pins. You should also try to keep the pins close to the seams, so that any pinholes that do show will be hidden.

*Sewing*. It takes a bit of practice to sew well on satin, and, as with all fabrics, I recommend that you practice on some scraps before you begin on the real thing. The problem with sewing satin is that it has a tendency to gather as you sew. This problem is similar to the problem with pinning; the satin surface is so slippery. However, this same slippery quality makes satin an easy fabric to turn inside out, which is something you'll be doing a lot of in soft sculpture.

If you plan on hand sewing, keep away from satin. As hard as it is to sew with the machine, eventually, with practice, one becomes accustomed to the difficulties and adjusts. The same is not true with hand sewing on satin.

There's just too much movement in the fabric for two hands to control!

*Durability*. Satin will hold up well if it is not put to constant use. You might use satin on a decorative pillow, but not on a pillow that people will actually be rubbing up against.

In many ways satin is a highly impractical fabric, as is so often the case with luxury items. It soils very easily; even water tends to leave rings on this lush weave. Also, because there is so much warp, satin tends to snag, and you need to be very careful handling it.

Finally, if the satin should require ironing, always iron on the wrong side.

*Cleaning*. Dry-clean only! Remember what I said above about satin and water. Yes, there are a few satins that claim to be washable (Qiana is one of them), but these fabrics are in a much higher price range, and despite manufacturers' claims, I'd still send them to the dry-cleaner's.

*In general*. At this point you're probably wondering what satin has in its favor. It's hard to work with, hard to clean, and hard to keep. Yet satin, believe it or not, is one of the most popular fabrics used in soft sculpture—and for very good reason.

Quite simply, satin is beautiful. Surely beauty in art is worth a bit of struggle. The surface sheen combined with rich, luxurious colors, makes satin the perfect medium for expressing fantasy. It stuffs easily, when you use top-quality stuffing, and it's truly a treat for the eyes.

### Pile

Pile fabrics are the ones that have a fuzzy, soft surface. You can probably think of them yourself, but I'll help: Velvet, velour, terry cloth (a looped pile), and corduroy are the most popular of the piles. By now, since you understand the concept of weaving, you can probably visualize the process by which pile fabrics are constructed. The pile is achieved when the filling (or horizontal) yarns are brought to the surface and cut. If you've ever hooked a rug, you've participated in the making of a pile.

*Characteristics.* Visually, the piles have a soft finish; they are generally used to achieve a gentle feel and luxurious look. Unlike satin, pile fabrics are as soft to touch as they are to look at. The nap looks different if you rub it one way than it does when you smooth it down, and you should make an effort to have the nap facing the same direction when you sew two pieces of fabric together. I remember when I was a child drawing letters with my finger on a favorite velvet jumper, and erasing them just by smoothing the fabric in the opposite direction with my hand. It wasn't magic—it was pile fabric!

*Workability.* The pile fabrics are very easy to work with, but there are certain precautions you must take if you are to work with them successfully. Because the pile has some depth, you'll find that when you lay the fabric face to face it will tend to shift a bit. Unlike satin, the pile fabrics won't slip and slide all over the place. They'll slip just the tiniest bit—just enough to foul up whatever you're cutting. This slipping is very easy to deal with, however, so don't despair. You simply must pin frequently and carefully. Pinning doesn't pose any problem with pile fabrics, as it does with satin, since the density of the fabric is more than ample to hide any pinholes.

Remember to make certain to lay the fabric with the nap running in the same direction. If you don't take this precaution, you'll end up with what appears to be a multicolored project!

*Sewing.* I warn you again: Practice sewing on some fabric scraps before you begin to work on the real thing. From playing with scraps you will arrive at the proper tension and stitch settings, and if all of these settings are right, you won't have any problem sewing.

Once you have set the knobs on your machine, pin, pin, and pin some more. The same shifting that can occur in cutting can occur in sewing, and it's terribly unpleasant to have to rip seams and straighten out little wrinkles in the fabric. Believe me, I know!

*Durability.* As a rule, the pile fabrics do not wear well. Velvet is particularly fragile, since it's a loose weave. Velveteen and corduroy, the tighter weaves, have a longer life. If you have a favorite old pair of corduroy pants, you know what these fabrics look like when they begin to wear. Check out the seat of your pants, and you'll notice that the raised section of the corduroy—the pile ribbing—is no longer raised. In fact, the pile is no longer there at all.

Another problem with these fabrics is that they tend to collect dust. You can try to vacuum them, but you risk some damage to the sculpture in the process.

Finally, pile fabrics do not hold up well under pressure—and I mean that quite literally. This particular limitation means that you cannot iron them on the right side. You can iron the wrong side of a pile, but are better off just steaming out wrinkles. You also might avoid placing the unabridged *Oxford English Dictionary* on top of a pile fabric—if you're inclined to do any such thing.

*Cleaning.* How you clean a pile fabric depends entirely on its fiber content. When you buy the fabric, ask what it is made of. Usually it will be machine-washable, but likely to shrink. To avoid any risk, it's best to dry-clean.

*In general.* The pile fabrics, despite their limitations, are very popular in soft sculpture. They look good combined with other fabrics—and provide an interesting visual and tactile contrast. They're most often used on personal objects like bags, jewelry, and pillows, because they're so nice to touch.

## THE KNITS

The only knit that I need address myself to here is the double knit. As you know if you've ever done any knitting or crocheting, you cannot cut a single-knit fabric. All of those loops, when cut, would unravel, leaving you with nothing more than a pile of tiny pieces of yarn. Double knits, however, are designed for precisely the kind of handling that soft sculpture involves. The bonded knits are not really flexible enough for our purposes. So let's talk in more detail about double knits.

### Double knits

A double knit is a fabric with two identical knitted layers that are connected and cannot be separated. Imagine the back and front of your sweater connected inseparably. You wouldn't have much of a sweater left, but you'd have a dandy example of a double knit.

This type of construction gives the fabric a great deal of stretch and body. The extra stretch and body prevent bagging. Remember the rule about not hanging sweaters in your closet, to prevent the shoulders from taking on the shape of your hanger? That kind of precaution is less necessary with a double knit.

*Characteristics.* Double knits look and feel like very firm fabrics. Occasionally they are a bit stiff, and this stiffness can make them inappropriate soft-sculpture material. You have to use your judgment. They're available in a wide range of colors, prints, and designs, but are usually more exciting to look at than they are to touch. They evoke feeling based on their surface design more than as a result of any inherent trait of the fabric itself.

*Workability.* As I have just said, you'll have to use your judgment about each individual piece of fabric when it comes to using double knits in soft sculpture. Since they are made from such a wide range of fibers, their stiffness varies. Often they are made from polyester blends, and often these blends are too stiff to take well to stuffing.

*Sewing.* There are several problems in sewing double knits, all of which can be overcome if you practice sewing on scraps first. The scraps should give you ample opportunity to set your pressure and tension. But even after practice, double knits may be a problem. They snag very easily, and sometimes the thread skips a stitch. You can nearly eliminate this problem by sewing with a ball-point needle and polyester thread.

The ball-point needle is preferable in this instance to a regular needle, since it slides over the yarn and into the holes created by the loop construction. A regular needle will pierce the yarn rather than enter the loop, and give the finished line of stitches a puckered, snagged look.

Polyester thread is *always* preferable to cotton thread. It doesn't shrink or break. For some reason I assumed precisely the reverse when I started doing soft sculpture, and spent a great deal of time rethreading my machine. Jerry straightened me out on the matter of thread, and you'll spare yourself the trial-and-error process of learning if you start with polyester.

*Durability.* The big plus for double knits falls in this category. They hold up well, wear well, and don't fade easily. Aside from the problem of attracting lint and snagging, these are strong, durable fabrics.

*Cleaning.* Again, double knits don't pose any more of a problem with cleaning than they do in terms of wear. They wash well in warm water, and they're dry-cleanable. I would offer one warning: Don't dry-clean printed double knits. If your fabric has a design, turn it to the wrong side to determine whether the design is woven or printed. If it's actually looped into the fabric, the reverse of the design will show on the wrong side. If it's printed on the face of the fabric, no design will show on the wrong side, and you'll find that dry-cleaning may dissolve the print.

*In general.* I must say that double knits are not my favorite fabrics, but they do occasionally fit the bill. I'm particularly drawn to double knits when I want a gold or silver lamé, for a piece of jewelry or trim. But the pros of double knits certainly cannot be ignored. If you're making something that will be handled a great deal, consider using this immensely durable fabric. If you'll be using a poor-quality stuffing—specifically, one that shows lumps and bumps—double knits are stiff and heavy enough to give any stuffing a smooth appearance.

## NONWOVEN FABRICS

Fabric, as I said earlier, is composed of fibers, and, one way or another, the fibers in fabric must be connected. We've talked about spinning the fibers into yarn and either weaving or looping the yarn. But there is still a third way of constructing fabric, which doesn't require the spinning process: compression. Compression is the oldest known manner of fabric construction, and the chief product of this process today is felt. Long before there were looms, people gathered the wool fibers used in felt, wet them in rivers, and pounded them together on rocks, under a hot sun, to create pliable, warm fabric. Wool fibers are particularly suited to the manufacture of compressed fabrics, because their texture is rough and grips easily.

Today, of course, the process of making felt is mechanical and much refined from the days of beating fibers on rocks. Still, felt is composed mostly of woolen fibers, occasionally combined with other natural and synthetic fibers, joined under heat, moisture (steam), and pressure.

Since felt is used so frequently in soft sculpture, and particularly in this book, let's examine it more closely.

### Felt

*Characteristics.* Felt has a soft-looking matte finish. The matte finish gives it a sturdy appearance, which is actually somewhat deceptive. It looks exactly the same on both sides, which eliminates any problem of wrong and right side in cutting and sewing. And felt is available in a wide variety of colors, either very bright or dull (the middle range of colors, for some reason, isn't available), though it doesn't come in any patterns.

You'll find, when you go to buy your felt, that it's available by the yard or by the square. While these small squares of felt can be limiting, they also make it possible to buy the full spectrum of colors for your project without amassing drawersful of leftover fabric.

Felt is not among the most flexible of fabrics, and usually its use is limited by its stiffness. It's too stiff to stuff tightly, and works best for small projects and details on other fabrics.

*Workability.* Felt is great fun to work with. It's easily cut with scissors or a sharp knife, and since it's not a woven fabric it produces a crisp edge that will never ravel and fray. When you cut felt with pinking shears the little points retain their shape. This technique of cutting felt can add an interesting decorative touch to nearly any felt project.

You'll also find that felt requires very little pinning. The somewhat coarse surface grips a like surface, and two pieces of felt placed together won't shift the way pile fabrics and satin do. Since pinning or basting takes time, the elimination of this step can cut project time nearly in half.

*Sewing.* Felt is easily sewn either by hand or by machine. Since it doesn't fray, you can use it for decoration without hemming the edges, and you needn't sew a felt project on one side and turn it inside out. It can be top-stitched—with either a plain or a decorative stitch—and stuffed. This technique is particularly useful on projects like the alphabet mobile, where the curves of the letter would make turning them inside out impossible.

You'll also find that you can sew closer to the edge of your fabric when you use felt without worrying about seam fraying. If at any point in your stitching the needle swerves in a bit from the seam line, you can trim around the outside edge when the sewing is completed and insure a uniform appearance.

Felt also lends itself to other forms of attachment, particularly to gluing. Since felt can be glued, you can always add some felt trim to a piece of sculpture as a decorative afterthought.

*Durability.* Felt is not among the most durable of fabrics. I don't recommend it for objects that will be handled a great deal, since handling tends to wear through the fibers and create thin spots or holes. Once there's a hole worn in felt, or if the fabric should be punctured, it's very difficult to repair in any way other than by applying a patch.

You also have to be careful about how you stuff felt. Since it's a very thick fabric, you can use virtually any kind of stuffing without worrying about a lumpy appearance. But the lack of elasticity implies a lack of softness. It's true that the fabric has a soft appearance, but that is a different matter from a soft stuffed look. You simply cannot fluff up a felt project the way you might fluff up a cotton one. Your best bet in stuffing felt is to go light on the stuffing. Never pack it in tightly.

*Cleaning.* Dry-clean only! You can never wash felt, and if you try you'll quickly discover that water can undo the entire compression process. Wet felt will eventually become a pile of fiber.

Keep in mind also that glue dissolves in dry-cleaning, and if you've used glue to attach any felt, you have made it virtually uncleanable.

Since felt attracts dust, it's a good idea to vacuum it lightly, or to clap your hands against it the way you might have clapped erasers in grade school.

*In general.* Felt is certainly not the perfect fabric for everything, but where it's right, it's more right than anything else. As I said earlier, you never have to turn it inside out, since there's no "right" side, and you can sew it, glue it, trim it . . . there's virtually nothing easier to work with. And it has a folksy, whimsical appearance. It's a favorite fabric of mine.

# Stuffings

An unstuffed piece of soft sculpture has about as much in common with soft sculpture as the pillowcases in your linen closet have to do with pillows—not very much. Obviously, the primary characteristic of soft sculpture is its stuffing, and before you start stuffing there's a lot to learn . . . to make it easier.

Your options with regard to stuffing are vast, but essentially all stuffings can be divided into three categories: fibers, foams, and miscellaneous.

The most popular and versatile of all the stuffings are fibers. These fibers—the basic component of fabric—are available either from nature (the natural fibers) or from chemistry (the synthetics). The most obvious of the natural fibers—and the one we are most concerned with here—is cotton. Cotton stuffing is, quite simply, cotton that has not yet been spun into thread. The synthetic fiber you will use most often is polyester.

Both of these fibers can be bought in three basic forms: loose, batting, and cording. Your concept of the sculpture you design will determine the form of stuffing you use. Essentially, these three forms are a convenience for you. Loose fiber stuffing is best used to fill a form after it's been sewn. If you were to open up the seam of your bedroom pillow you'd see that it probably is filled with loose fiber.

Batting is made in much the same way as felt. It is fiber formed into sheets, which can vary in thickness. If you lifted the fabric off your quilt, you'd most likely find a sheet of batting.

Cording is exactly as it sounds: a long tube of fiber encased by a net, which helps retain its tubular shape. It's often used on upholstery, to help define shapes and corners. Look at the furniture in your living room and see if you can find the covered cotton tubing.

All three forms of fiber stuffing are important in soft sculpture, and we use each of them in the various projects of this book. The more you work, the easier it will be for you to determine exactly when to use what.

The foam stuffings can also be divided into the natural and synthetic categories. The natural foam is, of course, rubber, and at the top of the list of synthetic foams is polyurethane. Both the natural and the synthetic foams are available in two forms: shredded and sheet. The shredded foams are used in much the same way as loose fibers, and the sheets correspond in their function to fiber batting.

The final category of stuffing is miscellaneous —by which I mean whatever you have around the house. And I really do mean "whatever." You can stuff fabric with almost anything: old nylons, fabric scraps, newspaper, down, sawdust, sand, Kopak, polystyrene, or dried beans. By no means is this miscellaneous category of stuffing to be considered less preferable. Of course, a bathtub toy stuffed with old newspaper doesn't make much sense, but there are times when something in the miscellaneous category will turn out to work better for your purpose than any of the other stuffings.

When I first made the fern pillow—one of the more complicated pillows in this book—I showed Jerry my finished piece and asked him for advice. The leaves all looked exactly as I had planned, but somehow the whole pillow didn't sit properly. He looked at the base of it and without a moment's indecision suggested that I stuff the base with beans, rather than dacron fiber. I redid the base as he suggested, and the pillow took on an entirely different look. It looked exactly as I had intended it to when it was nothing more than a fantasy of mine. The weight and texture of the base allowed it to balance over the arm of a chair, with the big fern leaves free to flop in every direction. In this case, beans were by no means "making do." They were the right stuffing for the project.

Just as there are questions you must ask before you choose fabric for a project, there is a series of questions to think about before choosing a stuffing. Most of these questions will become evident to you as I discuss the individual stuffings and their uses. But it is important to remember that you never choose a stuffing in a vacuum. The first thing you must always ask yourself about any stuffing is how compatible it is with your fabric. As I've said, if you've opted for a fabric that requires dry-cleaning, your stuffing cannot be one which is dissolved by dry-cleaning fluid. If your fabric is very sheer, your stuffing cannot be one that tends to lump. These precautions may seem terribly obvious to you now, but I assure you, there is no one making soft sculpture today who hasn't at some point overlooked the obvious.

## COTTON

You already know something about cotton as it is used in fabric. For a moment now, forget it. Let's get back to the beginning of cotton . . . the seed and the hair of the cotton plant. Again, this unprocessed, unspun cotton is available in three forms: loose, batting, and cording.

*Characteristics.* Loose cotton fiber is very soft-looking, and soft to touch, but it isn't very resilient. Resiliency is important in a stuffing. A fiber like cotton, which is lacking in resiliency, should be reserved for projects that require heavy stuffing. If the cotton inside your project gets flattened, it won't bounce back into shape as easily as some other fibers might with only a fluffing. On the contrary, it's likely to ball up and form lumps if packed lightly.

Cotton batting is similar to felt in basic structure and appearance, and is composed of compressed white cotton fibers. Although easy to use—it quilts easily—it, like the fiber, doesn't have much resiliency, and your quilting will have a flat look.

Cotton works best as stuffing when it is formed into a tube. Cotton cording can be purchased by the yard at a reasonable price, and makes the construction of coils, which you'll be doing a bit of, very easy.

*Durability.* As I said earlier, cotton fiber in its loose form has a tendency to clump. There are a few ways to get around the problem, but there's no way to actually avoid it. You should use loose cotton fiber only with a heavy outer fabric, like canvas. If the outer fabric is sheer, the clumping will show earlier. Also, remember when using loose cotton fiber to stuff tightly. Your project will have a harder look, but there may be times when that's exactly what you're aiming for.

Cotton batting has a tendency to depart from its original shape and shift between quilted layers. This can result in a lumpy-looking piece of sculpture. You can get around it with a great deal of top-stitching, but cotton is not the best choice for batting.

Cotton cording holds up well and is easy to use. The best way to work with it is to tape the ends before stuffing, but you needn't think about that now. Each project that involves cording will direct you in its use.

*Cleaning.* Cotton stuffing, in any form, can be washed so long as it's inside a washable fabric. If your outer fabric requires dry-cleaning, the cotton stuffing can be dry-cleaned. This means that, with regard to cleaning, cotton is compatible with all fabrics.

*In general.* Since it's been around longer, cotton has been in use as a stuffing for much longer than any of the synthetics. But slowly it is being replaced by the synthetics. Upholsterers are using dacron fiber now where they once used cotton. Cotton fiber has become difficult to find, and expensive when you find it. Its major asset is its bulk. It adds more weight than volume, and in certain objects this quality may be desirable. As a rule, though, with the exception of cotton cording, I don't recommend its use.

## DACRON

Since I've already told you that dacron fiber is taking the place of cotton fiber, you might assume that it is free of all the problems of cotton . . . and your assumption would be right. Dacron, which is made of the polyester filament, is the stuffing you'll be using most often throughout the projects in this book. It's available both as a loose fiber and in batting form, and in both instances is white and less dense-looking than cotton.

*Characteristics.* Dacron fiber is soft to look at, and generally soft to touch. Occasionally it's a bit scratchy, but even on those rare occasions when you come across a scratchy bundle, the texture deviation isn't great enough to interfere with stuffing.

Dacron batting is similar to cotton batting in appearance, but is so light that you can usually see through it.

*Stuffability.* Because of their great resiliency, dacron fiber and batting are the easiest of all the fibers to use. They don't lose their resiliency as you work with them, so it's never necessary to pack them too tightly. Generally, so long as your object looks filled, the less dacron stuffing you poke inside the better. Since it has so much more volume than weight, it's an ideal stuffing for large objects.

Dacron batting quilts well, is easy to use, and looks fuller than its cotton counterpart.

*Durability.* If you use a dacron filling, you needn't worry about clumping or about the shifting that's so much a problem with cotton. It holds up well through use, and if it does become compressed, you can easily fluff it up as you would any pillow.

*Cleaning.* The dacron fills hold up well whether you wash them or dry-clean them, and are therefore compatible with any fabric.

*In general.* In addition to its fine performance as a stuffing, dacron fiber is readily available and reasonably priced. It's sold by the pound in five-and-ten-cent stores and sewing centers.

## FOAM RUBBER

Foam rubber is a natural foam, structured around air bubbles. The density of the foam is determined by the size and number of air bubbles. Usually foam rubber is used in bedding, and in some furniture, and it is often used in combination with one of the fibers. The pillows of your living-room couch may have a foam core surrounded by fiber. The core accounts for a great deal of bulk and firmness, while the fiber wrapped around it give a soft feel and touch.

Usually foam rubber is sold in sheets, which vary in thickness and size. It's also available in a shredded form used in the same way as loose fiber.

*Characteristics.* Foam, shredded or in sheets, varies in color from white to beige, depending on the quality and age of the piece. It has a soft, dry coolness to touch, and ranges in appearance from smooth to heavy and spongy.

*Stuffability.* As I said earlier, foam rubber is at its best when you combine it with another stuffing, relying on the foam to add weight and bulk. It's difficult to work with in sheet form, because it cracks and tends to look hard and squared. There may be occasion for just such a look, but if you want a soft-looking piece of sculpture, you'll find it necessary to cover your foam with fiber. Also, because of its bulk, foam rubber is never a good stuffing for small, intricate objects.

*Durability.* Foam rubber doesn't hold up well. Old age approaches early, and the foam, whether in sheets or shredded, will crack and crumble. You can check the aging process of foam by using zippers in any foam-stuffed sculptures and examining the foam frequently for yellowing and dryness, but you're better off avoiding the problem entirely.

*Cleaning.* Foam rubber can be washed by hand in cold water, but cannot be dry-cleaned. *Never* cover foam rubber with a "dry-clean only" fabric, unless you're prepared to dispose of your sculpture when it gets soiled.

*In general.* A good rule of thumb regarding the natural stuffings—both cotton and rubber —is keep away. (The exception, of course, is cotton cording.) In every case, there is a synthetic that does the job better and with fewer problems. If you do decide to use foam in its shredded form, make certain that the outer fabric of your piece is thick, bonded, or quilted. This type of fabric, when stuffed with foam, will show fewer lumps and give a more evenly stuffed appearance.

## POLYURETHANE

Polyurethane is to foam rubber as dacron is to cotton. Some very helpful scientists examined all of the problems of foam rubber and set out to make a similar foam material without those problems. And they did a near-perfect job of it. It's available in both sheet and shredded form.

*Characteristics.* Polyurethane varies in color from white to yellow, depending on exposure to air. Yellowed material is no less resilient or in any way inferior to newer white polyurethane. Don't apply the same standards of color to this synthetic that you do to rubber. Old polyurethane may not be as white, but its performance is as good as ever. It is dry, cool, spongy to the touch, again depending on its density.

*Stuffability.* Shredded polyurethane isn't as heavy as foam rubber, but is equally voluminous. It's the perfect stuffing to add volume without adding weight. But it does have problems. Foremost among these problems is its static buildup, which makes it difficult to work with. It will attract all kinds of scraps, and stick to itself. If you keep your hands *slightly* damp you'll cut down on the static buildup, but you must take great precautions to differentiate between damp and wet.

In sheet form, polyurethane serves the same purpose as foam-rubber sheeting, and must be used with the same limitations in mind. It tends to look hard and square, and if you want a soft appearance for your sculpture, you'll have to soften the corners with fiberfill.

*Durability.* As I said earlier, polyurethane won't crack, mildew, or turn to powder the way foam rubber does. Although it yellows, the yellowing doesn't affect durability. And although it tends to stick to itself and form clumps, it can be fluffed up easily and resume its proper shape.

*Cleaning.* Like foam rubber, polyurethane can be washed by hand but not dry-cleaned. This limits the fabrics you use it with to the washables.

*In general.* Polyurethane is available in both sheet and shredded form at dime stores and sewing centers, and at very reasonable prices.

The key to successfully using this synthetic is to remember to stuff it somewhat tightly. If you fill the form well, the shredded bits of polyurethane are less likely to move around and clump.

## MISCELLANEOUS

Although I've already touched on the category of miscellaneous stuffings, they deserve some special attention. Let's not forget that the odds and ends that are included in this category are the stuff from which soft sculpture sprang. Rag dolls owe their shape to rags, and beanbags aren't much fun to toss around unless they're filled with beans. These stuffings—which are limited only by your imagination—can add a great deal of character to your work . . . and save you some money as well!

### Sawdust

Sawdust is good for tight shapes where softness isn't important. Sometimes, if packed tightly, sawdust will help add rigidity to shapes when you want them to stand upright. A problem with sawdust is that it tends to leak through the seams of your sculpture, so you'd be wise to make double seams when using this stuffing and to use a tightly woven fabric. Not washable.

### Sand

Sand is never really stuffed into a sculpture. Rather, it is poured in. It's very heavy, and acts as a good ballast. When using sand you must be certain that it is completely dry and clean. And, as with sawdust, you should use a tightly woven fabric and double seams to guard against leakage.

### Dried beans

Beans are one of my favorite stuffings. Of course, you can use them only when the design calls for them, but I like the feel of a beanbag. They're good to use as ballast—as are sand and sawdust—but beans don't put as much tension on the seams, and needn't be packed as tightly. Stuffing with beans tends to accentuate imagery. If, for example, you were making a stuffed frog, beans would be a perfect stuffing. The way they fall inside a sculpture gives the shape they are stuffing a sloppy, loose, and spontaneous look that changes every time you put it down.

There are a few problems with beans, however. This summer I made a pillow with beans and kept it in the living room of our cabin. We had some tiny field mice in the house that I never thought about until one morning I found my pillow, entirely emptied of its beans—a neat little hole nibbled into the fabric.

Another precaution you must take with beans is to keep them dry. Any moisture gets them ready for cooking, not stuffing.

Of course, bean-stuffed sculpture cannot be washed or dry-cleaned.

### Polystyrene

I learned about polystyrene around the time of my wedding, when some of my gifts arrived packed in it. It's a white synthetic packing material available in an assortment of shapes. The most common form is the small white pellets, which look very much like tiny pieces of styrofoam. It's a lightweight stuffing that's highly static, and for that reason messy and difficult to work with. Polystyrene is particularly good for large projects made with heavy outer fabrics. The huge beanbag chairs that were in vogue not too long ago were stuffed with these synthetic pellets.

Although they're difficult to get, they are available, and the best way to find them is to ask the manager of a store that uses them where he or she gets them. Of course, you can save them, or find someone who's getting married and collect them from her house every day as she opens her wedding gifts.

Polystyrene is neither washable nor dry-cleanable, so it makes little difference what fabric you choose to cover it with. The vinyl fabrics are most suitable for use with polystyrene, since they're heavyweight and can be sponged clean.

### Down

Down, the under-plumage of waterfowl, is the stuff that keeps you very warm, and doubles the price of your average ski jacket. It's an expensive, lightweight stuffing that's hard to find, and it flies all over the house when you try to work with it.

But, given all of this, there is something very nice about down on small luxury items. Specifically, it's soft, very nice to touch and cuddle, and pleasantly floppy in appearance.

Down must be dry-cleaned (even though it's from waterfowl, I wouldn't risk wetting it).

### Scraps

This is really the miscellaneous in the miscellaneous category. We can include old nylons, pantyhose, newspaper, fabric scraps, rags, T-shirts, and anything else you can conjure up. Of course, the uses of each of the things I've mentioned will vary. Old nylon stockings, cut up, give a soft, even appearance and are washable and fairly resilient. Old newspapers, crumpled or shredded, aren't washable or dry-cleanable, and will flatten with use. Stick to your common sense in judging these stuffings. If you use any cut-up old clothing, follow the washing instruction that you did when it was new. It's still the same fabric . . . recycled!

# Trimmings

"Imagination" is the key word when we talk about trimmings, and the important thing to remember is that there are *no* rules to follow!

Trimming adds an extra dimension to soft sculpture and can be part of your original concept. But the nice thing about trimming is that you can always add it as an afterthought to something that just doesn't look quite right . . . and transform it into something that's exactly the way you imagined it. The effect of a small piece of trim on a big piece of sculpture can be startling.

Basically, trimmings can be divided into two categories: functional and decorative. But since the categories are defined by application, they often overlap. Let's examine the functional trimmings first.

Generally, functional trimmings are fasteners: zippers, Velcro, buttons, snaps, hooks and eyes, etc. The vast selection of buttons at your notions store is evidence enough that trimmings like these can be decorative as well as functional. In fact, it's possible that you may opt to use a functional trimming in an exclusively decorative capacity. For example, you can use buttons as eyes on a rag doll, or a heavy-gauge zipper as the mouth on a soft jack-o'-lantern. Several years ago some of the most famous designers in Paris decided it was time for the hidden zipper to "come out," and all of those invisible, narrow garment zippers grew big teeth and shiny brass handles. Decoration is entirely subjective, and literally anything might work.

Which brings us to the decorative trimmings. In the broadest sense, they consist of virtually anything you can find and attach to the surface of your work that will enhance it. My sister-in-law recently had occasion to take apart an old lamp. She's an artist, and her mind works in creative ways, so she put all the small brass fixtures in an envelope for me, assuming that they might be useful as some sort of trim on one of my sculptures.

That's the way your mind should be working. Granted, such thinking results in cluttered, overcrowded drawers, but if you save things, a year from now you'll probably have exactly what you're looking for.

The most obvious decorative trimmings are feathers and beads. Feathers come in almost as many colors as there are birds, and are readily available. If you go to the fishing department of a sporting-goods store you can buy the kind of feathers used in making lures. You can take fancy big feathers off old hats, or ask your butcher for some chicken feathers.

Beads can be used alone or in combination with other materials. They can be made of wood, plastic, glass, or clay, and vary as widely in form as they do in material. They're readily available in notions stores, fabric centers, and the five-and-dime. And, of course, you can always "unbead" an old dress or necklace to recycle the trimming.

Ribbons are fun to work with, and they combine well with other trimmings. They can be knotted, tied, twisted, and curled, and they can be as functional as they are pretty. However you choose to use them, they're available in a vast variety of fabrics, weaves, prints, and colors.

Most of the trimmings you use can be purchased in a sewing center. But, at the risk of sounding redundant, shop around. Go to flea markets and thrift stores. You may find something special that's no longer being manufactured . . . and at a bargain price.

# The Projects

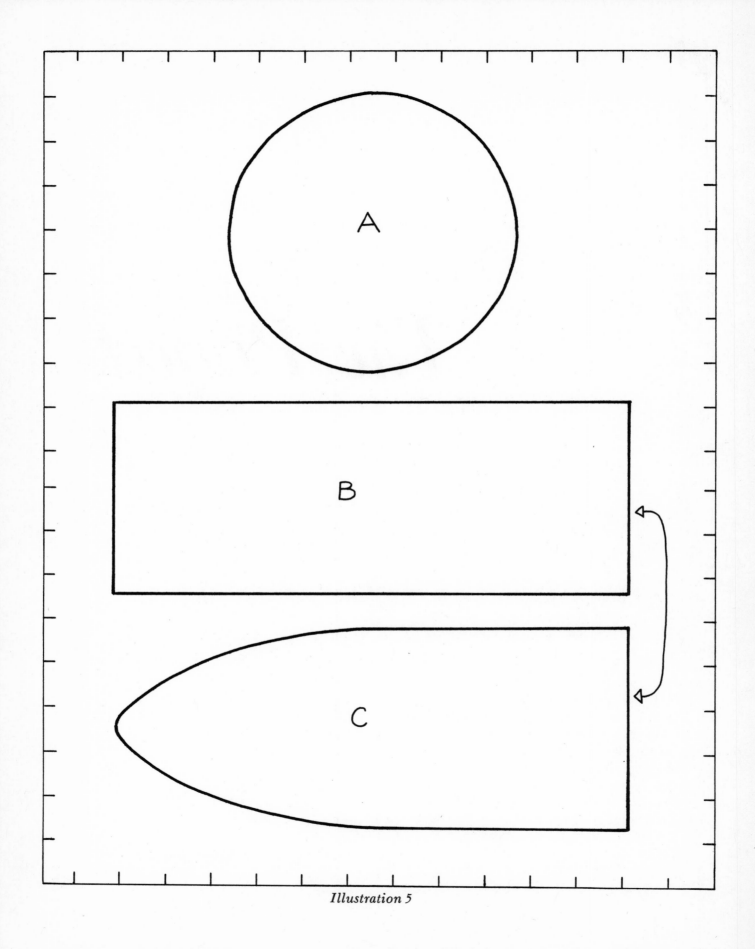

*Illustration 5*

# Pin Pincushion

Since this is your first soft-sculpture project, I felt that it had to meet several needs. First, it had to be easy enough for you to make comfortably. I promise you that this project will be fun to make, not a taxing chore. Second, I wanted to make the first project something you would be sure to use, and as you make your way through this book there's nothing you'll find more useful than a good-sized pincushion. Pins stuck in the wrong place can be quite uncomfortable! And finally, I wanted this project to capture the spirit of soft sculpture, and if you remember Jerry's preface you'll see exactly how the soft pin manages to do this.

Let me go over some of the thinking that went into this project. I thought of several different concepts for pincushions, a few of which I actually executed; and they worked well. The first cushion I made was in the shape of a whale. I began the project attempting to make an oversized spool, but somehow when I looked at the spindle of my spool it looked more like a fish. So I put two little beads on the face of it, sewed on lips (I know fish don't really have lips, but bear with my quirkiness), and experimented with some stitching on the back that turned into a tail. When I was finished, my spool had turned into a whale, and until I finished my pin pincushion, the whale was my primary pin depository.

Still, I wanted to try to make a soft spool. I kept working on my design, and finally turned the project over to Jerry, who worked out the kinks. While all of this was happening, I had the idea of a pin-shaped pincushion, and I liked that concept even better than the spool. It's particularly appealing since pins are hard, pointy, steely little things. Enlarging them and making them soft provides an interesting contrast. Jerry liked the idea and made a few changes in my initial soft-pin design, and together we arrived at the pincushion you're about to make.

My original pincushion was a green-and-white gingham. Jerry made it up in gray felt, and we both liked the verisimilitude the gray fabric suggests. Of course, the fabric you use is entirely up to you. Just be certain to read the chapter on fabrics very carefully before you make your choice. Remember that certain fabrics, like satin, don't take well to pinning, and would be a poor practical choice for a pincushion.

This is an inexpensive project to make and can be done in one sitting, which makes it an especially good idea for a gift.

## SPINNING OFF

Of course, there's a great deal you can do with this project by altering its size. If you fill in the grid lines around the tracing page, as I discussed in the chapter "How to Use This Book," you can blow the pin up to make a pillow, or a wall hanging for your sewing room. And if you reduce it and clip a pin on the back of it you can make a funky little piece of jewelry. Where you go with this soft pin is up to you.

## WHAT YOU WILL NEED

- 2 small squares of gray felt
- loose fiberfill stuffing
- cardboard or oak tag
- ordinary typing paper
- carbon paper
- gray polyester thread

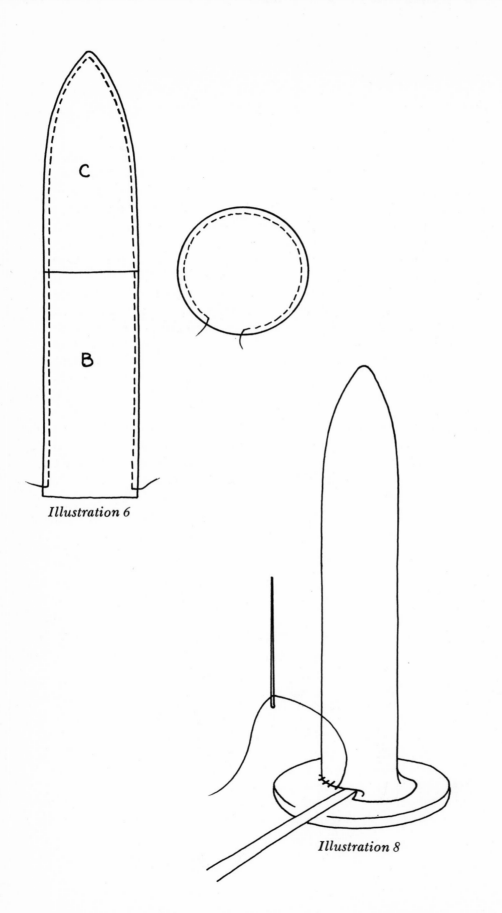

Illustration 6

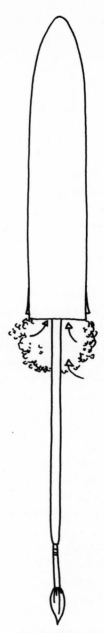

Illustration 7

Illustration 8

## MAKING THE PATTERN

Since I want to make this project as easy as possible for you, I decided to make the pattern traceable. The only problem in this case is that the shaft of the pin is too long to fit on the page of the book! But that's an easily solved problem.

In order to avoid complications, and save you the task of blowing the pattern up from a graph, I divided the shaft in two. (See illustration 5.) After you've followed my instructions for making the pattern, you'll have to attach both pieces of the shaft.

### Transferring the tracing page to paper

First, lay a sheet of ordinary typing paper over the tracing page and trace the outline of the circle. Then, lining up the bottom of your typing paper with the bottom of pattern piece B, trace that piece along the vertical of your paper. Lift up your typing paper and place it over pattern piece C, so that the bottom line of that piece overlaps with the top line of pattern piece B. (See illustration 6.) In this way you will be joining the two pieces of the pin shaft on your pattern.

### Transferring the pattern to cardboard

Now you'll need to transfer the paper pattern onto cardboard. First, get a piece of cardboard that's big enough to hold the entire shaft of the pin as you have just drawn it. I suggest that you buy a sheet of oak tag. Or look in your cupboard for a nearly empty cereal box, eat the remaining cereal, and then cut up the box. (It's always easy to find an excuse for eating.) Now lay the typing paper over the cardboard, keeping the design you have just traced facing you. Slip a piece of ordinary carbon paper, shiny side down, in between the two. (See illustration 2 in "How to Use This Book.") Draw over the lines you have just traced with a ballpoint pen. In this way, you will transfer the design onto cardboard.

When you have drawn both pieces of the pattern onto the cardboard, cut them out.

### Transferring the pattern to felt

Either lay one piece of felt on top of another or fold one piece in half, so that you'll be working with a double thickness of fabric. Pin through both layers of fabric to hold them together securely. (As I said earlier, in the chapter on fabrics, felt is a very easy fabric to work with and because of its texture it requires little pinning.)

Now lay the cardboard template of the pin shaft over your fabric and trace around its edge with a felt-tip pen. Repeat this procedure with the cardboard template for the circular pinhead.

## CUTTING YOUR FABRIC

With sharp scissors, cut carefully along the lines you have just drawn. When you finish cutting you should have two matching pieces of pin shaft and two matching pieces of pinhead.

## SEWING

You will be sewing with 1/4" seam allowances in most of the projects in this book. Most sewing machines have seam allowances marked on the plate below the needle, but 1/4" is always the easiest seam allowance to follow—simply use your pressure foot as a guide. All pressure feet are 1/4" wide, and if you line up the edge of your fabric with the edge of your pressure foot and maintain that line throughout, you'll have a perfect and even 1/4" seam allowance.

Now look at illustration 6 and sew your matching pattern pieces together—first the shaft and then the pinhead—following the sewing lines indicated. The openings will serve as your stuffing holes.

After sewing, remove your fabric from the machine and turn it inside out. Although felt has no right and wrong sides, we don't want the seam to show on the outside of the pin, so we have to turn the seam in.

## STUFFING

Before you begin to stuff, make sure to read the chapter on stuffings. It's always important to understand your materials before you begin working. For this project you will be working with a loose fiberfill stuffing. This stuffing is light and resilient and takes on the shape of whatever it's filling, so it's particularly appropriate for this sort of project.

Using your fingers, the handle of a paintbrush, a chopstick, or any long, somewhat pointed object as a tool, begin pushing stuffing into the hole you have allowed. (See illustration 7.) The important thing to remember about stuffing is to keep things soft. If you put too much stuffing in your sculptures, they'll look and feel hard, and, as I said before, the advantage of dacron fiberfill is its soft resiliency. Put a puff of stuffing into your pinhead. Pat the piece from hand to hand as you would a patty of chopped meat. Then put some more stuffing in and pat the piece again. This patting distributes the stuffing evenly. Keep repeating this process until the pinhead is filled, its shape is clear,

and it's soft to the touch. When it's finished, do the same thing with the pin shaft.

When you have finished stuffing the round pinhead, fold in the fabric on either side of the opening by 1/4″ and sew it shut with an overstitch. (See Stitch Glossary for illustration.)

## ASSEMBLING

Now that you have a stuffed pin shaft and a stuffed pinhead, you have to assemble them to make a completed stuffed pin.

Lay the pinhead down on a table and place the open end of the shaft (the unpointed end) down on it. Try to place the shaft as close to the center of the head as you can. Using your pointed stuffing tool or your fingers—whichever is easiest for you—tuck in the unfinished edges of the fabric from the shaft so that they don't show. (See illustration 8.)

Hold the shaft in place with your hand and take a careful look at what you have. You should see an overblown pin standing on its head.

Again using a small overstitch, sew the shaft of the pin to the head of the pin, carefully stitching around the perimeter of the shaft. With this step done, you have completed your first project. Fill it with pins so that you'll be ready to begin the next.

# *Pear Pillow*

The fact that this pillow is shaped like a pear has no significance other than the fact that I like pears. The important thing about this project is that it will give you some experience with a very basic technique in soft sculpture. You will learn to construct a simple stuffed shape. Once you've really mastered this technique, you'll have the skill to make and use complicated multipart patterns.

One very nice aspect of soft sculpture is that the beginning projects, like this one, are often as exciting to look at and as professional-looking as the more advanced projects. You need not worry, as in so many crafts, about having fifty saggy, lumpy-looking ashtrays, or a dozen long stockinette-stitch scarves. This pillow will be interesting and elegant.

If you feel a bit adventurous already, you might try some shape other than a pear. Perhaps another fruit or vegetable: apple, strawberry, banana? If you have confidence in your ability to sketch, draw your pattern freehand; if you're less sure of yourself, the following technique will allow you tremendous freedom. Cut out a picture of what you want to make from a magazine. (Make sure to find a picture that's clear and uncomplicated.) Cut out the shape you want to duplicate in fabric and glue it on a piece of ordinary typing paper. Then draw a grid over the picture and enlarge it as I've instructed for the grid designs in this book. Whatever the shape you decide on, the technique of enlarging a grid is the same.

I chose to make my pear from celery-green brushed denim. As with all of my projects, you can use any fabric you want. In this instance, as in later projects, I decided to go for verisimilitude in color rather than sheer whimsy. But there's no reason a pear-shaped pillow wouldn't work in a bright print, a velour, or polished cotton.

The leaf, which is optional, is a contrasting green brushed denim. Again, the choice is yours for the leaf fabric, but it should probably be consistent with the fabric on the pear.

The stem, once again aiming at a close representation of the real thing, is in brown brushed denim. You might try a rougher fabric for the stem than for the body of the pear, because stems do have a rougher look than the fruit itself. If you have a scrap of fabric from a sewing project, try making the stem from it. The highlights are just a detail, but I think they're very important to the total effect of the project. They add a touch of funkiness, which is really at the heart of soft sculpture.

## SPINNING OFF

There's a great deal to be done with this project, and using the very basic skills you learn from the pincushion. When I first thought of making a pillow in the shape of a pear, my thoughts went beyond the single fruit to a bowl full of various fruits. I've made up quite a few of them, following the basic techniques you'll use for the pear pillow. They really look splendid sitting together on the floor in a soft bowl. You can make a soft banana, a soft avocado, a soft orange, and so on. My favorite are soft grapes, which are a bit complicated but worth the effort.

If you decide to make this giant fruit bowl, I suggest you make the bowl out of coils, which you'll learn about in the chapter on making a coil pot.

Of course, your spinoffs can lean in the direction of miniatures as well as blowups. The reason we left the grid on this project for you to fill in is that you may decide to turn the pear into a tiny tracing project, and use the drawings as you use the other tracer pages in the book. The small pear can be a pendant, or part of a fruit mobile.

Big or small, this project is easy and fun, and bound to look good.

## WHAT YOU WILL NEED *

- 1 yard celery-colored brushed denim
- 2 8″ squares of contrasting-green brushed denim for leaf
- small scrap of fabric for stem
- 1 4″ square of white felt for highlights
- polyester thread to match fabric
- polyester fiberfill
- pins
- cardboard or oak tag

\* The amounts I've indicated for fabric will be adequate if you make your pillow the same size as mine. If you vary the size, wait until you have cut out your pattern, and use the pattern pieces to judge your fabric needs.

## MAKING THE PATTERN

### Enlarging the grid

Attach the lines around the rim of the pattern pages to form a grid.

Read the instructions for enlarging from a grid on page 9. The size of your pear pillow is entirely up to you, so you'll have to determine the scale of your enlargement. My unsewn pear measured, from top to bottom, 16″. If you want to make your pear the same size as mine, make each square in your grid 1¼″. I suggest making your grid on a piece of oak tag. You can cut up cereal boxes to get the right-weight cardboard, but oak tag (or poster board) is readily available, inexpensive, and easy to work with. After you transfer the pattern (the pear, the stem, the highlights, and the leaf) from my grid (illustration 9) onto your own, cut out the pattern

pieces. The leaf is optional, but I think it's a good touch. I have drawn the highlights on the pear with a dotted line to indicate their placement. Make certain to include them, in place, on your enlargement so that you know where to attach them.

When you finish cutting out your oak-tag templates, you should have the following: a full-size pear template; one leaf template; one stem template; and one highlight template.

## CUTTING THE FABRIC

Now that you've drawn and cut out your pattern, you're ready to lay out the fabric and transfer the pattern onto it. Fold the celery-green fabric, the dark-green fabric, and the brown fabric each in half, right sides together. You will be cutting through double fabric. Place each pattern piece over the appropriate fabric (pear on light green, leaf on dark green, stem on brown), and, while holding the cardboard in place with one hand, trace around the edge of the templates with a ballpoint pen. When you have traced each pattern piece, secure the doubled fabric by pinning inside the lines you have just drawn, lay the fabric on a flat, hard surface, and cut. Don't ever cut on a rug or a bed, unless you're prepared to replace shredded carpets and sheets.

When you have finished cutting the brushed denim, lay out the white felt and trace around the highlight template four times. Cut out all four white squares.

Remember: Cutting is the most crucial step in any project. If you take your time and are careful, there shouldn't be any problem. So don't ever feel pressured to rush through your cutting. It's helpful to take long cuts with your scissors, picking up as much fabric as possible with each snip. This method insures a straight line.

## ATTACHING THE HIGHLIGHTS

The advantage of making highlights out of

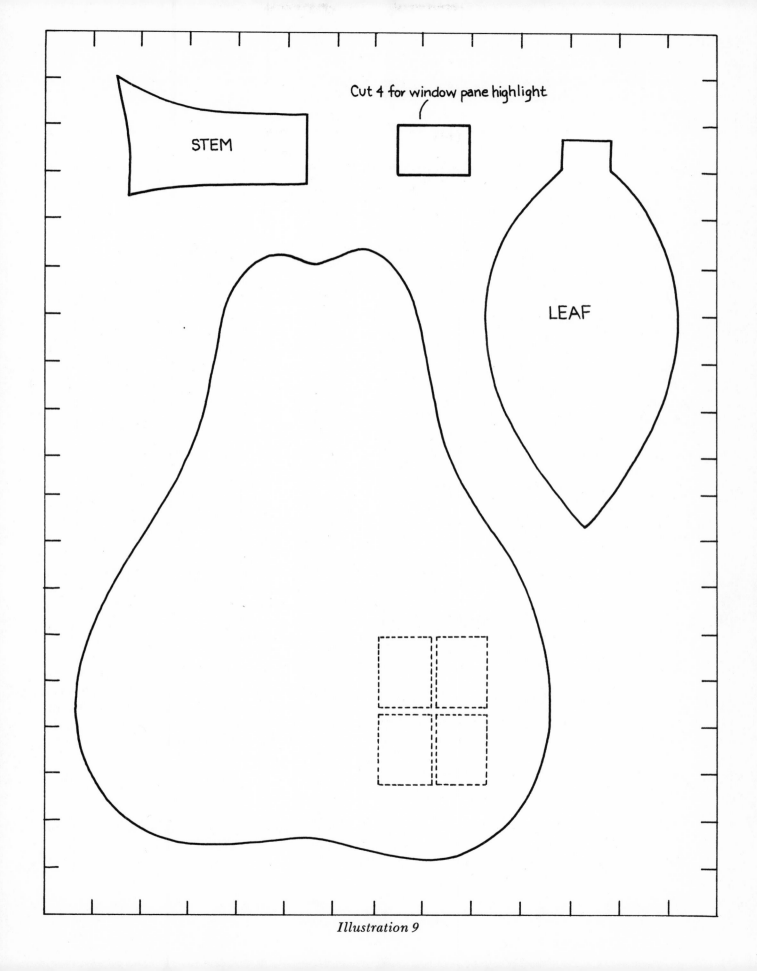

STEM

Cut 4 for window pane highlight

LEAF

*Illustration 9*

felt is that you don't have to fold in the edges and hem them before you attach them to the pear face. If you decide to use satin or another fabric besides felt, fold, press, and hem ¼″ in around the edge of each highlight before attaching.

Turn the front of the pear right side up and lay it beside the corresponding pattern piece. Arrange the highlights on the right side of the fabric as they're arranged on the template. You can do this easily by eye, and need not be too concerned about matching them perfectly with the pattern. Remember that the highlights represent light reflection, and, depending on where the light is, they could be anywhere on the pear. The important thing is to place all the highlights precisely as I did *in relation to one another*. They should form a little window, with each square representing one pane. Whether all four of them are a bit higher or lower on the pear is not important to the total effect.

With this said, pin the highlights into place and baste. Now set your machine at ten stitches per inch and sew each highlight on three sides (see illustration 10) making certain to keep the stitches very close to the edge of the felt. Take the pear out of the machine and push a small tuft of stuffing into each highlight. Don't overstuff in this case. We're only creating an illusion, and it has to be kept subtle. Remember, these are highlights we're making, not eruptions on the skin of the fruit!

After you've put a bit of stuffing in each highlight, put the pear back in the machine and sew up the fourth side of each square.

## PINNING THE FABRIC

Lay the two stems, the two leaves, and the two pears, each on top of its double, right sides together and pin along the edges. If you are going to be sewing by machine, make certain that the pins are perpendicular to the seam line.

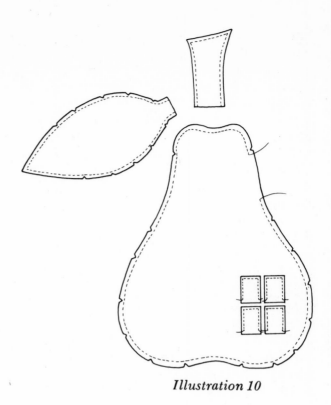

*Illustration 10*

## STITCHING THE PARTS TOGETHER

When you have pinned each part of the pear to its duplicate part, you are ready to begin sewing. Look again at illustration 10, which indicates stitching lines. You'll notice that each of the three parts, when sewn together, has a small hole in the seam, through which you will turn the piece right side out and push the stuffing.

### The leaf

The leaf will not be stuffed. Simply insert the pinned leaf pieces into the machine and sew as indicated, with a ½″ seam allowance. As you see from illustration 10, you will be leaving the bottom stem of the leaf unsewn.

When you have finished sewing around the perimeter of the leaf, notch the curves as indicated in the illustration. Then turn the leaf right side out through the hole in the bottom of the stem. Push a tool around the inside of the seam line, to make sure that none of the leaf remains folded in after you have turned it right side out. Your edges should always be sharp.

Since you aren't going to stuff the leaf, you can finish off the opening. Simply fold the rough edge of fabric approximately ¼", to conform with the seam line, and sew it closed with a small overstitch. (See Stitch Glossary.) Put your finished leaf aside for the moment.

### The stem

Insert your pinned stem into the machine and sew as indicated in illustration 10. You will be leaving the bottom of the stem unsewn, just as you did the bottom of the leaf. When you have finished sewing the three indicated sides of the stem, remove it from the machine and trim the excess fabric.

Turn the stem right side out. Unlike the leaf, the stem requires some stuffing. Poke a small amount of loose fiberfill into the stem. You don't want the stem to appear hard, so be careful not to overstuff. This filling is resilient, and a little bit of it will stuff a long way. When you feel that your stem is adequately stuffed, sew the bottom closed with a simple running stitch. (See Stitch Glossary.) You needn't bother to fold in the raw edge of the fabric, as you did for the leaf, since this end of the stem won't show on your finished pillow. Just sew the opening closed to lock the stuffing inside the stem.

### Inserting the stem

Before you begin to sew the back and front of the pear together, you have to insert the stem. The stem should be placed at the top of the pear. Take your pinned pear and remove the pins from the top curve. Insert the stem between the two layers of light-green fabric, with the top of the stem facing the bottom of the pear. (See illustration 11.) This may all seem upside down to you, but when you turn the finished pear right side out the stem will pop up as it should. Insert the stem far enough into the pear so that the rough edge of the fabric is aligned with the edge of the light-green fabric of the pear. Pin the stem in place.

### The pear

With your stem pinned in place, you're ready to sew together the back and front of the pear pillow. Place the fabric into the machine, and insert the needle at either side of the stuffing hole as indicated in illustration 11. Sew around the entire perimeter of the pear, allowing ½" for the seam, and make sure to sew through the stem. When you have finished sewing, remove the pear from the machine and notch the edge as indicated in the illustration.

Now turn the entire pear right side out, through the opening you have left on the side. Your stem, if attached as I directed, will pop out on top. When your pear is turned completely right side out, you're ready to stuff.

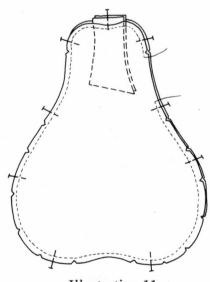

*Illustration 11*

## STUFFING THE PILLOW

It will take quite a bit of loose fiberfill to stuff your pear pillow, but, as always, you must be careful not to overstuff. I suggest that you poke a handful of stuffing into the pear through the opening on its side and then pat it into place.

Poke another handful of stuffing into the pillow, and toss the pillow from hand to hand as though making a meatball. Continue this process until your pillow is filled yet soft.

When you think you have enough stuffing in the pear, sew the side opening closed with an overstitch, just as you did the bottom of the leaf. Fold the raw edge of the fabric in approximately 1/4" to conform with the seam line, and sew it shut with a small overstitch. (See Stitch Glossary.)

## ATTACHING THE LEAF

Your pillow is nearly finished. If you decide not to have a leaf on your pear, the pillow is actually completed. But if you decide to attach the leaf, as I did, you still have to sew it to the stem. This is a very easy process and should be done by hand.

Sit the pear on your lap and hold your leaf. Bend the stem of the leaf lengthwise and wrap it around the pear stem as indicated in illustration 12. Secure the leaf in place with a few stitches as indicated in the same illustration.

The leaf should fall over the side of the pear and cover the hand stitching of the stuffing hole. With this bit of trim done, your pear pillow is finished.

## THE FINISHED PILLOW

The pear pillow looks great on a couch or chair, but I especially like the way it looks when you mix it with other soft fruit. You might want to go back and reread the section on spinoffs, and begin this project again . . . with a new slant.

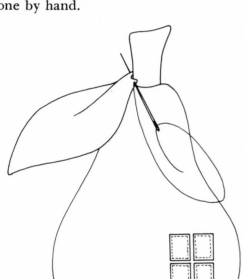

*Illustration 12*

# Name Mobile

Surely nothing makes a gift more personal than a monogram or an embossed, embroidered, engraved, or painted name. These days people are ironing their names or messages on T-shirts, aprons, baby quilts . . . everything. The basic ingredient of a name or message, is, of course, the alphabet, and, as I'll discuss later, this project offers you dozens of alternate projects. My instructions here put soft letters to a very specific, very special use—as part of a name mobile.

Mobiles are often hung above babies' cribs, because they're interesting to look at, and, I suppose, since a baby has little more to do than lie on his or her back all day, the area above a baby's bed should be made as interesting as possible. But there's no reason why a mobile can't hang in a doorway, above your own bed, over a table, even in your office, or any other place that you might appreciate looking at it. Remember Alexander Calder, who's actually credited with inventing the mobile? Perhaps an alphabet mobile seems too whimsical to be taken seriously, but the emphasis in Calder's sculpture is on fun, and fun can certainly be beautiful.

I like the idea of hanging my name mobile in the doorway of a child's room. But if you want a bit of variation on a theme, you might spell out a label: KTCHEN, OFFICE, QUIET. Use your imagination. The potential for stuffed letters, either huge or tiny, is vast.

I've discovered that felt is the best possible fabric for sewing stuffed letters, particularly if you don't want to make them very big. The bigger the letters, the easier it is to vary the fabric. This is because letters, with all their curves and angles, cannot be easily turned inside out, and therefore require top-stitching. (Refer back to the section on felt in the chapter on fabrics.) Top-stitching means, simply, that the article will be sewn together on the right side and the stitches will show on the finished letter. This stitching can be very attractive and is often used as a decorative device, particularly if you sew with a contrasting-color thread. You can even use the line of your top-stitching as a guide for more interesting embroidery. If you decide not to use felt, you'll have to hem the edges of each letter first, so that no unfinished edges show on your completed piece. This is a simple procedure: just turn in the edge of the letter ¼", baste, and hem.

I also chose to cut my letters with pinking shears. Since felt doesn't unravel and cuts cleanly, pinking shears will leave a crisp zigzag edge, which adds to the folk quality of the mobile and doesn't detract from its readability. If you don't have pinking shears, don't do much sewing, and don't anticipate a career in soft sculpture, don't bother to buy them. They're quite expensive, and although your letters will look different with straight edges, they will still look good. The alphabet I have given you to trace is very simple in its design, and straight-edge letters would certainly be esthetically consistent.

Another advantage in the choice of felt as the fabric for this project is that it comes in a wide variety of colors, and each color can be bought in small quantities. Most fabric stores sell felt by the square rather than by the yard, and you'll be able to make your mobile gaily multicolored, as I did mine, without filling your closets with leftover felt. But read my chapter on fabrics before you make any final decisions.

You can hang your letters on virtually any

kind of cord you like. If you want the letters to appear as though they're floating, look for a thin, invisible cord. Fishing line is usually a good choice. Since I was more concerned with color than with the floating illusion, I decided to hang my letters from silk macramé cord. This cord is inexpensive and readily available at hobby stores. I've used it on other projects, and you'll find it especially useful when you make soft jewelry.

## SPINNING OFF

This is an easy project, with vast potential for spinoffs. My instructions for creating a soft alphabet can be applied in a number of ways. You can use the grid to make big soft letter pillows or to make very small initial pendants. You can write out soft messages as gifts and decorate them with beads and bells. You can make a mobile like the one you're about to make, but have it hang from long knotted macramé cords. In fact, you can combine a host of crafts on this project. You might consider replacing the wooden dowels on this mobile with clay if you have pottery know-how.

Whatever you finally do with these soft letters, they're fast and very easy to do, and make nice gifts.

· I've already discussed some of the things you can do with the alphabet, fabric, and some stuffing. But let's consider here the possibilities of mobiles. The late Alexander Calder, "father of the mobile," was particularly fascinated with the idea of sculptures that moved. He made one of his mobiles and asked his friend Marcel Duchamp what he should call such things. Duchamp is credited with having dubbed the sculptures "mobile." But Calder didn't really invent the concept of mobiles. They've been used in folk sculpture in one way or another for centuries. Think of all the old whirligigs and weather vanes with hanging, moving parts. The variations are infinite. And even when you make mobiles with fabric you're confronted

with an infinite number of possibilities. You needn't use letters at all. Perhaps you'd rather substitute fruit. Or you might make a child's mobile with a big "A" and things that begin with that letter: apple, airplane, automobile, anchor, etc.

Read the section in "How to Use This Book" on using a grid. If you learn this skill, you will be able to take things from any magazine and make simple stuffed versions of them, to be put on a mobile or anywhere else.

Also, think about the other projects in this book. You have complete instructions for a pear pillow. If you follow those instructions, but scale it down to mobile size, you'll have the beginnings of a fruit mobile. You can make the cloud from the rainbow necklace and a bunch of stuffed stars, and *shazaam* . . . you'll have a heavenly mobile.

And remember, you needn't limit yourself to one main dowel and three hanging dowels. Look at some of Calder's mobiles in an art book. So long as you get things to balance, you can make as many levels as you want on your mobile. The more you put on, the more interesting it will be to look at, and the greater the potential for movement.

## WHAT YOU WILL NEED

- felt squares—at least 1 per letter
- polyester fiberfill
- pinking shears (optional)
- typing paper
- ruler
- polyester thread
- cardboard or oak tag

## MAKING THE PATTERN
### Enlarging from the grid
Follow the instructions in "How to Use This Book" for enlarging a grid. Look at the alphabet in illustration 13. If you want your finished mobile to be the same size as mine, each square on your enlargement should be approximately

$5/8''$, with the letters enlarged $3\frac{3}{4}$ times. Make certain to draw your enlargement on a piece of typing paper to facilitate tracing it onto cardboard. After you have drawn each of your enlarged letters, cut them out of the cardboard carefully. These cardboard letters will serve as your templates. Don't throw them out when you finish your project; you never know when you'll need that letter again.

## TRANSFERRING THE PATTERN TO FABRIC

Lay two pieces of felt together and pin around the edges. If you want a letter to be the same color on each side, make both layers of felt the same color. If you want each side of a letter to be a different color, pin together two different-color felts. Once the fabric is pinned, lay a letter over it and trace around the edge with a ballpoint pen, felt-tip marker, or soft pencil. Felt doesn't bleed, so you can use virtually anything when you draw on it. When you have made a clear, solid line, cut along it carefully, either with regular scissors or with pinking shears. You will be cutting through a double layer of fabric, so you should end up with two pieces.

## PINNING

When you have cut each letter that you'll be using, in duplicate, pin the duplicate letters together in preparation for sewing. These letters probably aren't very big, and you need use only a few pins to secure the proper alignment. As usual, remember that felt generally requires very little pinning, since its fabric surface holds firmly.

## PREPARATION FOR HANGING

It's not yet time to explain the hanging procedure for your mobile in great detail, but it is time to make a basic decision and to prepare for hanging.

If you have decided to hang your letters from macramé cord, as I did, you have to cut the cords and pin them to each letter now, before you sew the backs and fronts of each letter together. Look at illustration 14 and choose one of the three plans for hanging. You can devise some plan of your own, depending on how many letters are in the name you're making, but I've offered the three basic alternatives.

Once you have selected a plan for hanging, take note of the length of the cords coming from each letter, and cut your cords accordingly. Tie a knot at one end of each cord and slip the knotted cord between the two duplicate letters you have pinned together. Make certain that you pin the cord at the top center of each letter as in illustration 14. If you use this same spot as a stuffing hole, you will not actually stitch the cord into place until later.

## SEWING

Basically, you should use your common sense to decide where stitching lines belong. If you leave only one end open on a "Z" you're obviously going to have a hard time getting the stuffing all the way around to the other end.

It's up to you to pick a thread color. You may decide, as I did, to use the same color thread on all of your letters. I must admit that my primary motivation was that I hated the idea of rethreading my machine and changing the bobbin every ten minutes. Perhaps you're less lazy than I am.

## STUFFING

As in any felt projects, the major caution in stuffing these letters is: Don't overstuff. If you're making a large pillow of some fabric other than felt, you can push the polyester fiber in to your heart's content (although I can't imagine why anyone would want a rock-hard pillow.) But since these letters are small, and since they are made of a particularly nonelastic fabric, stuff them very lightly. Using a probe tool (chop-

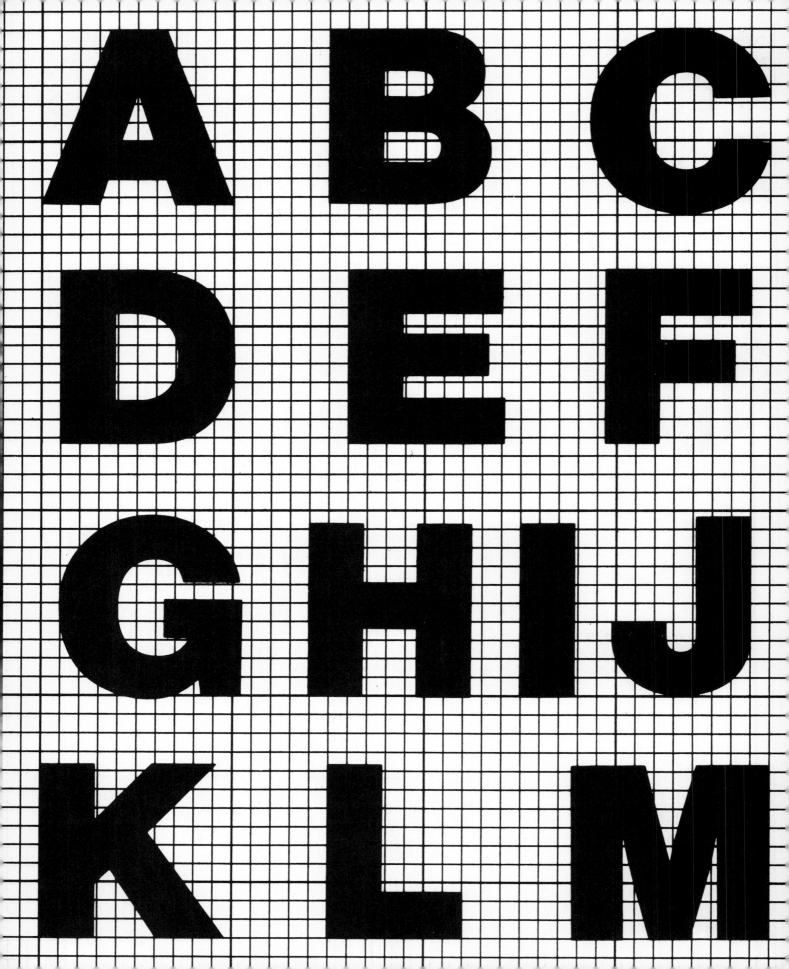

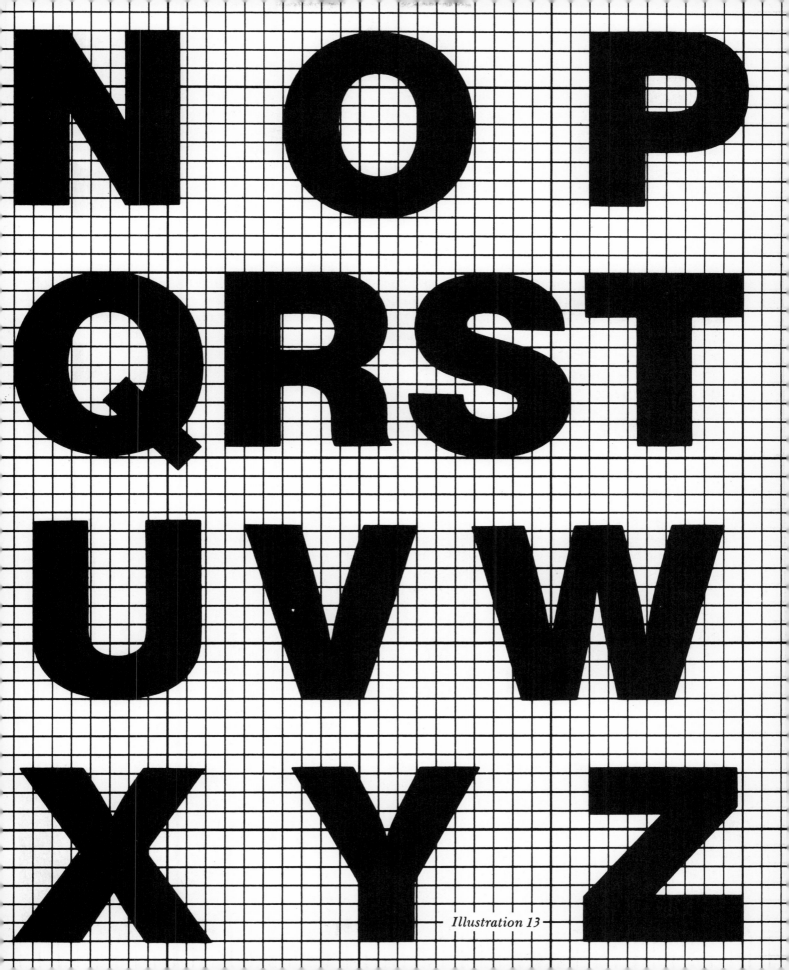

*Illustration 13*

stick, long handle, etc.), push small puffs of your polyester stuffing fiber into each letter. (See illustration 7.) Make sure to get some stuffing inside curves, close to the seam line, as well as into the middle of each letter.

When you feel that a letter is sufficiently stuffed, insert it once again into the machine to stitch the open ends. (In many cases you will be sewing through the cord as well as closing your letter.) This may be a bit tricky, but if you haven't overstuffed there should be enough fabric near the edge of your pressure foot to grab, and sewing should be easy. If you can't seem to get the stuffed letter into the machine, finish off the letter by hand with a small simple running stitch. (See Stitch Glossary.) Try to size your hand stitches so that they will match the machine stitching.

## HANGING

There are lots of different ways you can hang your letters. You may, as I said earlier, end up rejecting all of my hanging plans and creating one of your own. But the way you hang your letters will basically be determined by where your mobile is hung. If you hang the mobile on a wall, I suggest that you follow Plan A shown in illustration 14. This plan allows the letters to lie flat against the wall, with minimal movement, which assures best readability. Depending on the size of the room, this may be your best bet. I find that this plan is also best when I hang the letters in a doorway. Plan B is good for short names. The letters will spin around more than they do in Plan A, but movement is still somewhat limited. In Plan C you are assured virtually no readability, but are guaranteed lots of movement—which may be your primary concern. Let me explain in greater detail the construction of each hanging plan.

### Plan A

In each of the following hanging plans you will need a straight, stiff material to use as your horizontals. You can unwind wire hangers and

cover them with fabric, or you can go to your local hobby shop, hardware store, or lumberyard and buy the thinnest wood dowels available. I chose to use wood dowels on my mobile. For Plan A you will need one dowel 36″ long.

You can leave the dowel in its natural state, paint it, or cover it with fabric. Covering it with fabric, the most complicated of your alternatives, is the one I chose to do . . . so I'd best explain the procedure.

Simply cut a piece of felt that is 2″ longer than the dowel, and approximately 4″ wide. Fold the felt in half lengthwise and pin. Now sew a straight seam line ½″ in from your fold, down the entire length of the fabric. Trim close to the seam line with regular scissors or pinking shears, for whichever look you think will go better with your letters.

Now take your dowel and slide it into the casing you have just made for it. Close off each end of the casing with hand stitches after you have inserted the dowel.

Attach the cord that will run to the ceiling (or wherever you plan to hang your mobile) by tying a knot on one end and tying the other end around the center of the dowel. Follow the same knotting procedure for attaching the stuffed letters to the dowel. (See illustration.)

### Plan B

This alternative method of hanging your letters is a bit more complicated, but the procedure is the same. Using either a small sword or a serrated-edge knife, cut your dowel to 20″. Then cut two more pieces of dowel, 12″ each.

Cover each of these three dowels with fabric as instructed for Plan A. Attach the cord from which the mobile will hang to the center of the large dowel by knotting it around the covered wood. (See illustration 14, part B.) On each end of the large dowel attach another piece of cord, cut according to the diagram for Plan B, and knot the end of each of those two pieces of cord to the center of each small dowel.

Finally, attach the letters to both small dowels as indicated in the illustration.

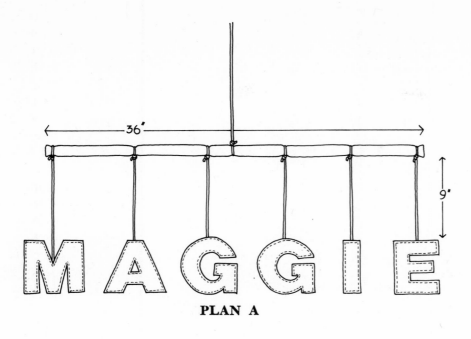

**PLAN A**

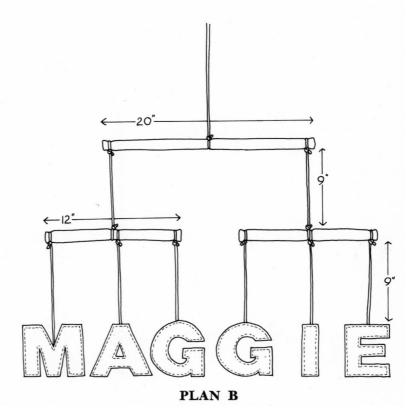

**PLAN B**

*Illustration 14*

## Plan C

The procedure for this plan is similar to that of the others. Cut your dowel as indicated in illustration 14. The large dowel should be 24″ long, and the three small ones 6″ each. Divide your letters evenly among three dowels this time, instead of two, and cover dowels with fabric. Attach cord as indicated.

## POLISHING UP

When you have done all of your knotting and your mobile is finished, you will need to polish a few rough edges. Go over the entire sculpture with a sharp pair of scissors. Check each of the knots and trim away excess cord. Trim the felt throughout the mobile so that it is close to your various stitching lines. The mobile should have a neat, polished look.

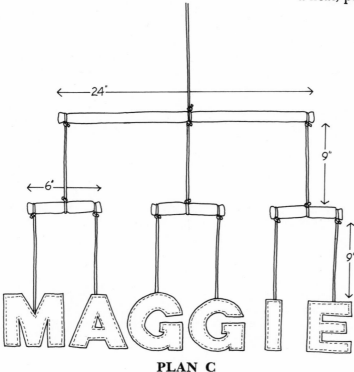

### PLAN C
*Illustration 14*

# Rainbow Necklace

## A Jerry Kott Design

Rainbows are magical, and the power of their magic has been reflected in theater, movies, novels, paintings . . . in the mythology of our culture. Jerry Kott has given up the fantasy of finding a pot of gold somewhere over the rainbow, but has translated his fascination with the natural phenomenon into a very special soft pendant.

Originally Jerry made the cloud-and-rainbow pendant in satin, with silk cord. He had hoped the satin would work for the piece because it's durable and fancy. But his experiment with a satin cloud was disappointing, for the very reasons we like satin on so many of the other projects. Clouds are soft; satin is hard. "For a leaf, which has a naturally hard, waxy surface, satin is fine," Jerry explained, "but clouds should look puffy and soft." Finally he decided on white felt for the cloud. Felt has precisely the soft surface he was looking for, and is very easy to work with if you're sewing around curves. It's true that felt is somewhat less durable than a woven fabric, but, when faced with the choice of durability versus esthetic appropriateness, Jerry opted for the latter. Besides, if you take some care with the pendant, there's no reason it shouldn't last. While it's true that felt isn't the most durable of fabrics, it's not fragile either.

The cord that Jerry recommends for the rainbow chain is commonly known as "silk macramé cord." It's readily available at hobby and fabric stores. "I like this particular type of cord," Jerry explained to me, "because it's really alive in color and works well as an exciting contrast to the matte finish of the felt." The colors he chose are those traditionally used to represent the colors of the rainbow: red, orange, yellow, green, and blue. Of course, you can use any combination of colors that you want for the chain, but if you stray too far from traditional rainbow colors you may confuse your end effect.

The price of silk cord isn't too high. Don't be put off by the word "silk." Jerry Kott has seen it priced anywhere from 10¢ to 50¢ a yard. Shop around. Also, you may be able to buy it only by the yard, not by the inch. If that's the case, don't be concerned about buying extra. It never hurts to have more to play with. You may discover that you want your pendant to hang lower than we suggest. And you can use leftovers to make a simple macramé bangle bracelet.

### SPINNING OFF

Because we've provided you with a grid on all of the traceable projects, there's virtually no limit to the number of spinoff projects you can make from this pendant. Jerry suggests making the cloud a bit smaller and shortening the silk cord, thereby changing your pendant into a choker. Or you might try cutting out a circle of yellow felt, to represent the sun, and attaching it almost anywhere—to the rainbow or to the cloud itself. You can string tiny beads and let them hang from the upper seam of the cloud like rain. Or, to alter the effect, you can use different thicknesses of cord. But beyond all of these alterations is the potential for real variation. Blow the cloud up so that it covers a wall (perhaps the wall above your bed) and use very thick cord for the rainbow. Hang it as you would any wall hanging.

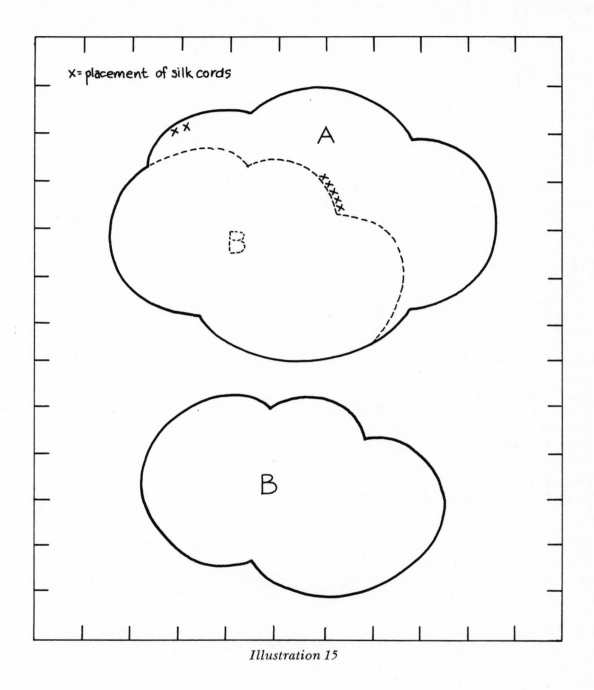

x = placement of silk cords

A

B

B

*Illustration 15*

STITCHING AND STUFFING

## WHAT YOU WILL NEED

- 8" square of felt (white or the color of your choice)
- silk cord: 14" each red, orange, yellow, green, blue, 12" white
- dacron or polyester fiberfill
- light-blue polyester thread
- Scotch tape
- cardboard or oak tag
- typing paper
- carbon paper

## MAKING THE PATTERN

The pattern for the rainbow pendant has two pieces: the cloud and the overlay cloud. On the tracing page (illustration 15) we've drawn each pattern piece separately, and indicated with a dotted line precisely how the overlay should fit on the cloud. We've also indicated the position for the rainbow and the white silk cord.

### Transferring the pattern to paper

Take a piece of typing paper and lay it over the tracing page. You should be able to see our lines through an ordinary piece of typing paper. Trace first the main cloud and then the overlay. You need not mark the overlay's position or the attach points of the chain. When the time comes to attach these parts, the proper placement will be evident if you glance back at the tracing page.

### Transferring the pattern to oak tag

Now place the typing paper, with your cloud outlines, over the oak tag. Put the carbon paper between the pattern and the oak tag with the shiny side of the carbon paper facing down on the cardboard. With a ballpoint pen, follow the lines you've just traced from the tracing page. Cut the cloud and the overlap carefully around the lines you have just drawn. Label the cloud A and the overlay B.

### Transferring the pattern to the fabric

Fold your felt so that it's double thickness and lay pattern piece A over the doubled fabric. There is no right and wrong side to felt, so you need not be concerned with how you've folded it. Hold the pattern template down with one hand, and trace around its edges with either a ballpoint pen or a soft pencil. Lift the template and pin the two thicknesses of felt together securely, placing the pins inside the line you've just drawn. Cut carefully on the line through both layers of felt.

Now unfold the remaining fabric and, on a single thickness of felt, repeat the above procedure for pattern piece B. We need only one piece of fabric for the overlay, since it functions as a surface ornament and a stationary point where the rainbow begins.

When you've completed cutting out your fabric you should have three pieces of cloud-shaped felt: two pieces of pattern piece A and one of pattern piece B.

## PREPARING THE CORD

Lay a small (1½") piece of Scotch tape on the table, sticky side up. The tape will help to position the cord and make it easier to handle.

Lay the ends of the cord over the center of the tape in the following order: red, orange, yellow, green, blue. (See illustration 16.) Make an effort to lay each color very close to its neighboring color on the tape. After the cords are positioned securely on the tape, fold the ends of the tape over on the cord, locking it into place. Now set the rainbow aside.

Take the 14" piece of white silk cord and tie a single knot at each end. Fold the cord in half, so that the two knots meet, and tie a third knot about an inch down from the fold. (See illustration 17.) This third knot should form a loop at the end of the folded cord. Set the white cord aside.

## SEWING

Now, with all the project parts prepared, we're ready to sew. Set your machine at 12

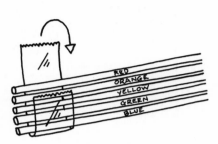

*Illustration 16*

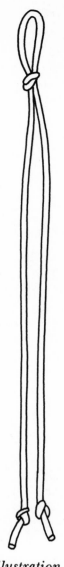

*Illustration 17*

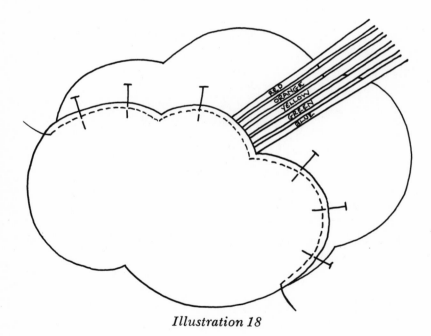

*Illustration 18*

stitches per inch. If you're sewing by hand, keep the stitches small and tight. Jerry has chosen a light (sky) blue thread for this project, which works beautifully with the cloud design.

Put one piece of pattern part A aside for later use. Pin the overlay on the second part A, positioning it as it is on our tracing page. When the cloud and overlay are securely pinned, slip the taped end of the rainbow between them at the point indicated in our drawing. Position the rainbow so that the taped edge almost reaches the bottom of the cloud. This will prevent you from stitching through the Scotch tape.

Place the assembled rainbow, cloud, and overlay into the machine with the overlay and the rainbow facing up. Begin at left, and stitch along the dotted stitching line as indicated in illustration 18. Sew as close to the edge of the overlay as possible, and sew slowly. The stitching is part of the design and it should be straight and even. Make sure that the silk rope is smoothed and in proper order as you sew over it.

### Stuffing the overlay

You have completed sewing the front of your pendant and are ready to stuff it. (Don't worry. We haven't forgotten that you have another pattern piece!) Before you begin stuffing, look carefully at what you have made. The overlay (pattern piece B) should form a pocket with pattern piece A. The end of the rainbow is now sewn inside the pocket, and there should be a small piece of tape, rather than a pot of gold, at the end. Trim the rainbow, eliminating the Scotch tape. After you have clipped the taped section off, put small amounts of the stuffing fiber into the pocket, poking it gently first into the curves of the cloud and then into the middle. (See illustration 7.) *Do not* pack the stuffing in. If you use too much stuffing it will distort the original shape of cloud, and you'll have trouble matching the back to the front. If you use a small amount of stuffing you will achieve a subtle, soft look.

Now, with the front finished, you're ready to sew on the back.

### Sewing the back

Take the duplicate pattern piece A and pin it onto the back of the big cloud. Make sure that the edges line up evenly. Slip the two knotted pieces of white silk cord between the matching pieces of felt as indicated on the tracing page. Pin securely and sew around the perimeter, allowing about an inch on the bottom for your stuffing hole. Again, sew slowly and close to the edge. The pendant is too small and curvy to race your machine. Take special care as you sew over the white cord.

### Stuffing the back

Now stuff the back through the opening, just as you stuffed the front: with a minimum of stuffing pushed carefully into the curves, and a final puff in the middle. Place the stuffed pendant in the machine and close the area of seam you left open for stuffing. Try to match your stitches evenly with the stitches you already made. There should be no evidence of your stuffing hole in the finished pendant.

## FINISHING TOUCHES

You've almost reached the end of this rainbow.

Pull all the silk cords of the rainbow together carefully and tie two knots at the end, the second knot over the first. The two knots should form a ball, which will act as a button.

The loop you made earlier at the end of the white cord will be your buttonhole. Push the button through the buttonhole and wear it around your neck.

This is not a very formal piece of jewelry, and I've found that it looks best when worn with a heavy turtleneck sweater. However you choose to wear it, it's a designer piece.

# Auto Mirror

This mirror is small, and much more decorative than it is useful, but it reflects enough of your face so you can put on some lipstick, and it's such fun to make that I wanted to include it here. It can be made in one or two sittings, which makes it an especially attractive project.

I decided to make the car out of felt because it cuts and glues so easily. Don't substitute fabrics this time. By the time you've finished making this project you'll understand why I like working with felt. Even if you can't sew a stitch, you can do all sorts of elaborate things with felt and glue.

I wanted to make a hanging mirror with more character than a simple rectangular frame. By now you're halfway through this book, and I'm sure you can figure out how to make a soft rectangular frame by yourself. Jerry and I spent an hour or so arriving at a shape. We tried to think of objects that had windows, with the ultimate idea of substituting a little compact mirror for the glass. For example, one of our ideas was to build a small house and substitute two small mirrors for the two front windows. Eyeglasses were another possibility. The car was actually the last thing we thought of, but it excited me most, perhaps because my first venture in soft sculpture was in the shape of a car. We decided to construct a frontal view of a car, and to use a mirror in place of the windshield. I thought I'd like to include all sorts of details, like the grid on the radiator, the fender, the headlights, and we decided that felt would accommodate all the detail work with the least amount of effort.

The outcome of all of this brainstorming is the auto mirror you're about to make. The finished project, as you see it in the photograph, is our own "custom job" car. If you look carefully at the photograph you'll notice some details that add to its funk. For one thing, it has an actual miniature license plate. If you read my chapter on trimmings you'll remember that I mentioned the value of being a compulsive saver. Years ago, the Disabled Veterans Association used to send tiny license-plate key rings when they solicited contributions. For some reason I saved a few of them. When I made this project I discovered exactly what I had been saving them for. You may not have this exact trimming, but you certainly don't need it to complete the project. Look for alternatives. Think about making a license plate entirely out of felt. Or you might consider cutting a headline out of a newspaper and gluing it on the fender as a bumper sticker.

The little plastic charm that I've glued to the top of the radiator came from a Cracker Jacks box. Please don't feel compelled to eat through a crate of Cracker Jacks until you find the charm. The charm I've attached actually interferes with the mirror, but I liked it so much that I decided to dispense with my pragmatic sensibilities and ride with whimsy. Usually decisions like that pay off.

## SPINNING OFF

There are several directions in which you can spin off from this project. You can, as always, alter the size of the car we've provided. If you're really adventurous you might want to make the car as big as four feet high and hang it on the wall of a child's room. Just fill in the grid we've begun on the tracing page and follow the instructions for enlarging in "How to Use This

Book." If you make the project that big, you'll have to take special care in attaching the mirror. Elmer's glue won't be strong enough to hold a large, heavy mirror.

You may also decide to make a miniature hanging mirror in some shape other than a car. I've already offered a few suggestions for alternatives—a house, eyeglasses—and you'll probably think of others. Keep in mind that you can always go to a glass-and-mirror shop and have a mirror cut to your exact specifications. If you have a cardboard pattern, the glass cutter (if he's good) will have no problem. If you're especially ambitious, you may decide to cut the glass yourself. I must warn you, though, that I was once that ambitious and the results were disastrous. Not only were my hands cut, but I had tiny slivers of glass on my floor for months.

Finally, you can vary from my pattern on the trim. I've already given you a few suggestions for variations in this area, but don't let my suggestions limit you. You can use some of your other craft skills, like embroidery, to decorate this project. You can embroider on a license plate, a bumper sticker, or whatever else comes into your head.

Whatever you decide to do, there's very little you can do wrong. Even if your seam line curves in a bit, you can call it a dent!

## WHAT YOU WILL NEED

- 1 square of yellow felt
- 1 square of gray felt
- 1 square of white felt
- 2 squares of felt (your color choice) for car body
- a compact mirror
- Elmer's glue
- loose fiberfill for stuffing
- cardboard or oak tag

## MAKING THE PATTERN

Lay regular typing paper over the tracing pages (see illustrations 19 and 20) and trace around the heavy black outlines of each of the six pattern pieces. When you have traced around the outlines of the car body, the headlight rim, the headlight, the fender, the tire, and the radiator, lift the typing paper. You may need more than one piece of paper to trace all six parts.

Now lay the typing paper over a piece of oak tag or cardboard. Slip the carbon paper between the typing paper and the oak tag. (See illustration 1.) With a ballpoint pen, transfer the pattern pieces onto the cardboard.

When all the pattern pieces have been transferred to your cardboard or oak tag, cut them out.

At this point you may notice that the radiator on the tracing page has stripes on it, and that in the photograph of my finished mirror there are strips of gray felt glued to the white radiator. You don't really need a pattern to cut these strips, and I'll instruct you on them later.

## CUTTING THE FABRIC

By the time you're ready to cut out fabric, you will have decided on just what color felt is going where. I suggest that you pick your favorite color for the auto body, and the following for the trim: tires—gray or black; headlight rims—gray; radiator—white; radiator strips—gray; headlights—yellow; fender—gray. Lay each square of fabric out on a flat surface to prepare for cutting.

### Radiator

Place the cardboard pattern piece on a single layer of white felt and trace around its edge with a soft pencil. Lift the pattern and cut.

### Radiator strips

This is the detail I mentioned earlier that doesn't require a pattern. Simply cut eight thin (approximately ¼″ wide) strips of gray felt. Make the strips approximately as long as the ones indicated on the tracing page, but don't worry if they're a bit long. You can always trim

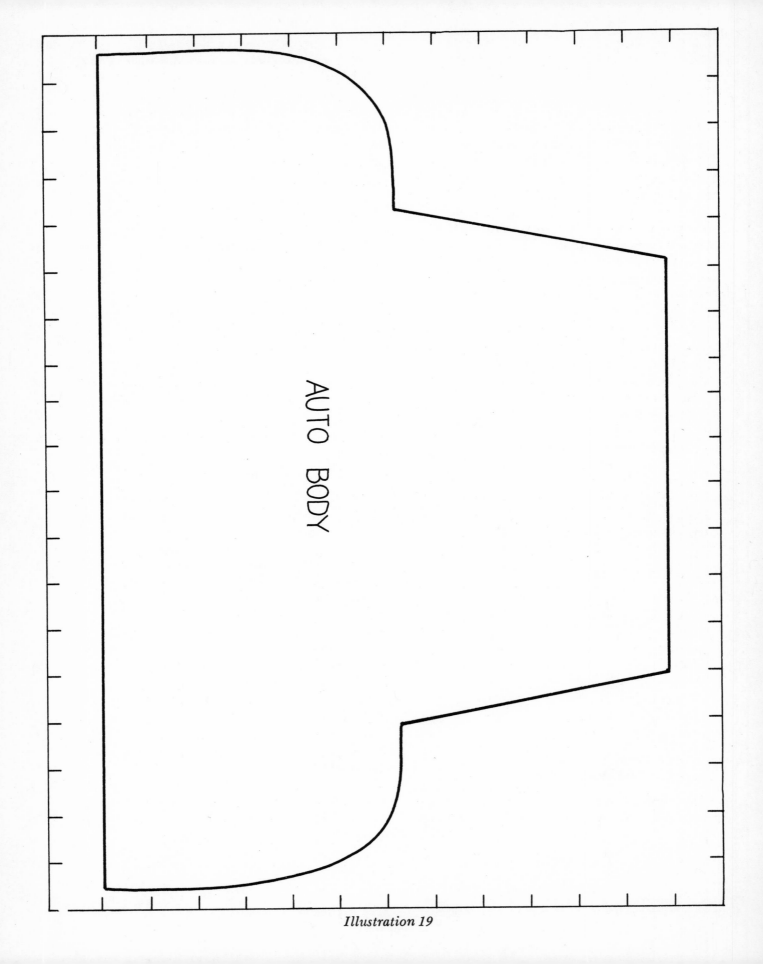

*Illustration 19*

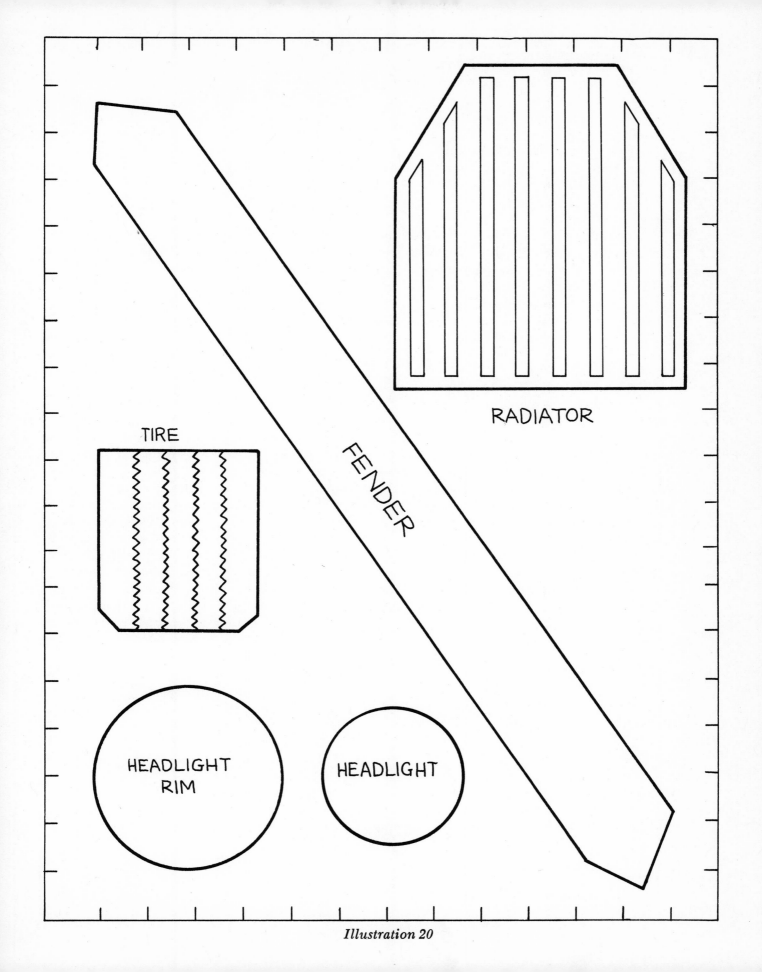

RADIATOR

TIRE

FENDER

HEADLIGHT
RIM

HEADLIGHT

*Illustration 20*

them later, and the bottom edge of the radiator will be covered by the bumper anyway, so irregularities won't show.

### Fender

Place the pattern piece over a square of gray felt and trace around the edge as you did for the radiator. Lift the pattern and cut.

### Tires

Lay two pieces of gray felt together and pin them, or fold one piece of felt in half. You need to work with a double thickness of fabric on each of the following pattern pieces, because we want to cut them in duplicate.

Lay the cardboard tire template over the doubled fabric, trace around the edge, and cut.

### Headlight Rims

Place the cardboard pattern piece over doubled gray fabric, trace around the edge of the pattern, and cut.

### Headlights

Put the smaller cardboard circle—the headlight pattern—over a double thickness of yellow felt. Trace around its perimeter, as you have done on the other pattern pieces, lift the cardboard, and cut.

### Auto body

Lay the cardboard auto body over a double thickness of the felt you have chosen. Trace around the edge and cut.

## SEWING

Before you actually sew the car together, there's a bit of preparation.

### The tires

There are several ways to make the gray felt tires you have just cut look more like tires than they do now. A simple solution to this problem is to take a black felt-tip pen and draw several zigzag lines down the vertical of each tire. This trim will look like the tread on a new tire. If you have a sewing machine that does a zigzag stitch, you can sew the tread into the tires, as I did. Look at the photograph of my finished project. The stitched-in tread looks more realistic than drawn-on tread. Even if your sewing machine doesn't sew a zigzag stitch, if you're handy with a needle and thread you can apply some of your embroidery skills to the tires and sew the zigzag line in by hand. If you do decide to stitch in the tread, I suggest you use black or gray thread.

### Pinning the tires to the body

Now that you've indicated the treads on each of your tires, you're ready to sew them to the body of the car. To simplify construction, you can do this at the same time you sew the front and back of the car body together. Lay the two pieces of car body over each other and pin them together.

If you look carefully at your tires, you'll note that one end of each tire is squared off and the other end has the corners trimmed. This trimming will create the illusion of roundness on the finished tire. Let's call the trimmed end of each tire the tire's bottom. Insert the tires in between the two layers of felt car body as indicated in illustration 21. Note that the tire bottom—the side with the trimmed corners—should be facing the roof of the car. Allow approximately ½″ of the tire to extend beyond the bottom of the car. Pin each tire in place.

The tires should be positioned as they are in illustration 21, but basically you can use your eye to determine where they look the most realistic—a bit to the left or right. Remember, the tires are being tucked between the two layers of felt, and will reappear when the car is turned right side out.

Now you're ready to sew the car together.

### Sewing the car body

Look again at illustration 21, this time focusing on the stitching lines around the perimeter

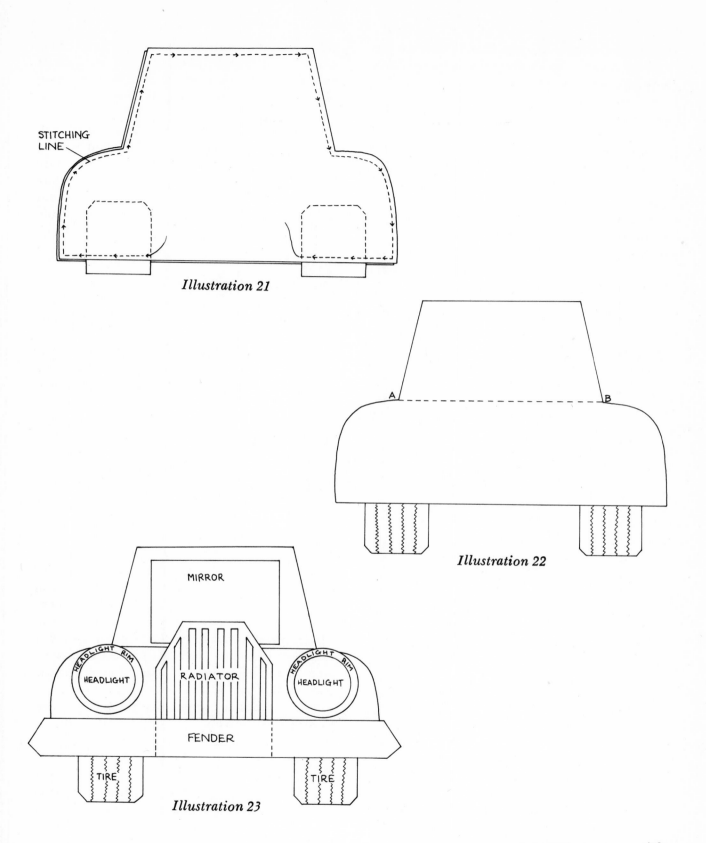

STITCHING LINE

*Illustration 21*

A                    B

*Illustration 22*

MIRROR

HEADLIGHT RIM

HEADLIGHT

RADIATOR

HEADLIGHT RIM

HEADLIGHT

FENDER

TIRE

TIRE

*Illustration 23*

of the car. Insert your car body into the machine with the needle directly above the inner side of the left tire. Allowing ¼″ seam allowance, sew in a clockwise direction around the edge of the car, following the stitch line, until you sew through the second tire. Remove the car from the machine and turn it right side out through the hole you've left between the tires.

By this time you've had lots of experience turning things right side out and you shouldn't have any problem. Push along the seam lines from the inside with either a chopstick or your fingers. With the right side of the car facing out, your tires should be visibly hanging from the bottom.

### Separating the top from the bottom

With the perimeter of the car sewn and the car turned right side out, you're nearly ready for stuffing. But in order to create an illusion of depth, you'll want to stuff only the bottom half of the car. In order to achieve this illusion you must sew the top of the car closed. With the right side of the fabric facing out, insert the car into your machine. Refer to illustration 22 and insert the needle at point A. Sew a straight line of stitches from point A across to point B. Remove from the machine.

## STUFFING

This is an easy project to stuff, since it's basically a simple rectangle with no hard-to-reach corners. Just push your fiberfill into the car through the unsewn area between the tires. (See illustration 7.) Remember not to pack the stuffing in tightly. This is a soft sculpture we're making, not a car of steel!

After you have finished stuffing the bottom half of the car, fold the fabric at the seam opening in ¼″ to conform with the seam line, and sew it shut with a small overstitch. (See Stitch Glossary.)

## GLUING

Now for the fun! Although I've provided you with a pattern for all the essentials of a car front, when you get involved with cutting and gluing you may decide to add a few of your own touches. But let's start with what we've got.

### Radiator

Spread a thin line of Elmer's glue on the back of each gray felt radiator strip, and one by one press them into place on the white radiator. You might look at the tracing page for exact placement of the strips, but felt is an informal, fun sort of fabric, and you needn't worry about duplicating my arrangement exactly.

When the strips have all been attached to the radiator, spread glue evenly on the back of the radiator and over the area on the car body where you will be placing it. Again, if you want to check exact placement of the radiator, look at the photograph of my auto mirror, or illustration 23, but it's basically a matter of eye and common sense.

The important thing to remember is that you should glue the radiator only to the bottom—stuffed—part of the car. The top of the radiator will be free-standing, and will add to the illusion of depth I discussed earlier.

### Headlights

Spread glue evenly on the back of each of the yellow headlights and glue each one directly over the gray headlight rim. Try to attach the yellow circle directly in the center of the gray circle so that a thin gray line rims each circle of light. The gray background is supposed to look like the chrome that circles headlights on most cars.

When you have glued the headlight to the headlight rim, spread the glue evenly on the back of each headlight rim and put a dab of glue on either side of the radiator (see illustration 23), where you will be attaching the lights. Again, check the photograph of the finished car for approximate placement.

### The fender

Spread glue evenly over the entire length of the fender and spread a thin line of glue across the bottom of the car, over the radiator. The bottom half of the fender can hang down, unglued, a bit beyond the bottom of the car, depending on how much room you have (See illustration 23.) You'll probably have some leeway here, and so long as the gray bumper strip doesn't interfere with the headlights you can place it by eye.

### The mirror

Last but not least is the raison d'être of your little car. The mirror should fit nicely on the top, unstuffed portion of the car. Spread glue evenly on the back of the mirror and on the fabric where you will place it, and press them together. Since the mirror is heavier than the fabric, press down for a minute to allow the glue to set. Try to center the mirror on the top portion of the car. (See illustration 23.)

### FINISHING

Your car is basically finished. You need only affix some sort of loop on the back, from which it will hang, before you can attach it to a wall.

I suggest that you go to your notions store or sewing center and buy a large hook and eye. You won't need the hook, but affix the eye to the back of your car. This metal loop is a secure way to hang the little car from a nail in your wall.

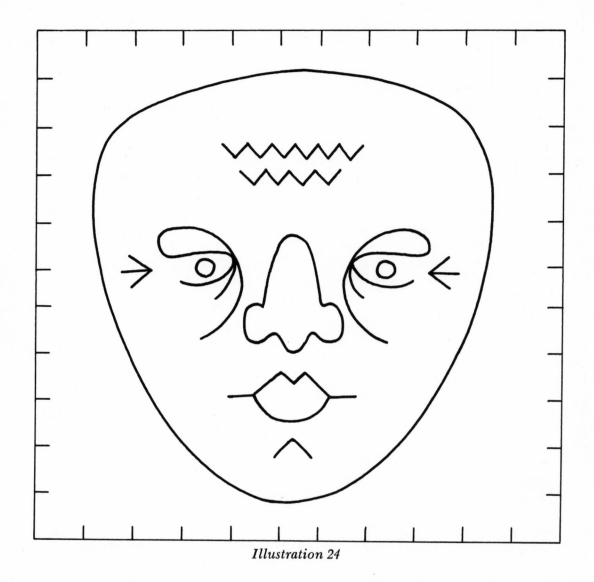

*Illustration 24*

# Face Belt

Probably anyone who has sculpted in any medium has at some point attempted to sculpt a head. When confronted with a glob of clay, most first-timers will pat it into a ball and pinch out a nose. There are heads in all the metals, wood, plastic, glass, marble, even in rubber. Such a sculptural tradition makes the idea of a fabric head seem almost obligatory. Soft sculpture certainly lends itself to realistic molding. Fabric is pliable, can be bent and fastened and stitched, and accepts the shape of whatever is filling it. Like other mediums, fabric can have a wide variety of finishes: soft, hard, shiny or matte. And since we're particularly concerned with the practical application of soft sculpture, I decided to make my soft head into a buckle, attach the buckle to a soft, shiny piece of macramé cord, and pull it through the loops of a denim skirt.

Don't let the idea of reproducing a face intimidate you. For one thing, the face you create need not be a photographic replica of a human face. Its proportions can vary. The placement of features can vary. (Remember Picasso?) And keep in mind your built-in familiarity with the subject. You gaze at yourself in the mirror daily, scrutinizing which features you like and which you don't. Most people can respond in an instant when asked about their least-favorite feature, and the response is usually greatly detailed. "My nose is too wide at the base and too thick at the bridge," you might say. You put makeup on your face and draw very careful lines and shadings to accentuate the good or diminish the bad. Trust me. You're more familiar with constructing a face than you think you are.

But still, starting from scratch for the first time is a problem. And I've provided a sure-fire solution to the problem in the shape of a traceable face, which will make this impressive-looking project particularly easy. All the lines are there for you to follow, if you want to. If you prefer to sketch your own character, by all means do.

The second piece of my belt is a simple macramé cord. You can substitute almost any kind of band for the belt, and might consider using the fabric coil I discuss in the chapter on making a coil pot.

Since I wanted my belt to be informal, and to suit many different outfits, and since I wanted to color parts of the face when I finished my sewing, I chose to construct it from canvas. The stiff fabric responds well to shaping, and it doesn't bleed when I touch a Magic Marker to it. I did my first face in muslin, which achieved the same effect as canvas but was too soft to really hold a shape.

But, as always, my choice of fabric is just a recommendation. You might use satin on your belt, with interesting results. It's something I'd like to try for a more formal look, to wrap around a pair of crepe evening pants or a slinky chemise. And you can color in the features with embroidery stitches rather than Magic Marker if you're after a more elegant look.

You'll need very little fabric for the face buckle, and may decide to use some scraps you have left over from a sewing project, in which case your face may be striped or checked. Anything *is* possible.

As always, I suggest you read through the entire project before you begin, and don't rush.

## WHAT YOU WILL NEED

- ½ yard fabric for face
- 60″ heavy silk macramé cord
- polyester thread
- polyester fiber batting
- pins and small needle
- typing paper
- sewing-tracing paper
- different color felt-tip pens
- iron-on facing
- cardboard or oak tag

## MAKING THE PATTERN

Put a piece of ordinary typing paper over the tracing page (illustration 24) and with a felt-tip pen trace the lines onto your paper. Make sure to include the square around the face when you make your tracing. Lay the paper with the newly traced lines over the oak tag and transfer the square to the cardboard. (See illustration 1.) Cut out the cardboard square and put it aside for the moment.

Lay out your fabric and with a felt-tip pen trace around the cardboard square three times. Cut out the cardboard squares you have just drawn on the fabric. In this project, as in several others, I suggest that you cut your pattern on the bias. This means simply that you must look closely at the weave of your fabric. There will be horizontal and vertical threads crossing one another to form a screen. To cut on the bias, turn the fabric so that the threads all run diagonally and cut after you've turned the fabric. (See illustration 4.)

Put aside one of the three squares you have just cut.

## TRANSFERRING THE TRACING PAGE

Buy a package of sewing-tracing paper at a fabric or notions store. This tracing paper will serve a similar function to that of carbon paper. You will use it to transfer the lines of the face to the fabric in the same way you just used carbon paper to transfer the square around the face to oak tag. This special tracing paper comes in packages at your sewing center, with several colors to choose from. I suggest that you use a color that contrasts with your fabric, but not too sharply. If you're using white canvas, as I suggest for this pattern, you might use yellow tracing paper.

### Ironing the facing onto the fabric

Before you begin to trace the pattern on your fabric, use the square cardboard template and one square of iron-on facing the same size as your squares of fabric. Following the instructions on the package, apply the iron-on facing to the wrong side (if you're using canvas there is no right or wrong side) of the fabric. Generally, the iron should be dry, set for cotton, and left over the unglued side of the facing for five seconds.

Apply the facing to only one square of fabric. This will give the back of your buckle some extra stiffness but leave the front soft for molding.

### Pinning for tracing paper

Place a square of fabric (other than the one with the iron-on facing) on a hard surface. Put a square of sewing-tracing paper directly over the fabric, colored side down. Lay the sheet of typing paper with the face over the colored tracing paper. (See illustration 2.) Secure the three layers with a few pins around the edge. Redraw over the lines of the face and over the oval outline with a ballpoint pen. Press down hard enough to insure that the lines will be transferred to the fabric. You might test the entire process with scraps before you begin. When you've gone over all of the lines of the face, unpin the layers and put the square of fabric aside for the time being.

Now take the fabric square with the iron-on facing and place it, facing side up, on your table. Arrange the yellow tracing paper over it, colored side down, and place the pattern over the tracing paper as you did before. Thus far you have duplicated the last procedure. This time, however, draw over only the outer oval of the face, thereby transferring it to the iron-on facing. Unpin your layers and set the square of fabric aside.

When you're finished, check the fabric. One square should have a light outline that looks exactly like the face on our tracing page. The other square should have only the oval outline of a face, directly traced over the iron-on facing.

Now that the lines are drawn, you're almost ready to begin sewing.

## BATTING

In this pattern I use batting rather than stuffing to achieve a smoother, more even look. Later, if you want some extra padding in the nose, you can always add it. But the overall face is shapely enough with just the original batting. Double the thickness of the batting, lay the cardboard square over it, and cut around the edge.

## SEWING

If you've done everything according to instructions so far, you're ready for the fun part of this project. Since the face is small and the features will require some detail, I suggest you do most of the sewing by hand. If you feel very confident about yourself on the machine and think you can accurately follow the lines you've drawn, then try sewing by machine. But I advise against it. Machine stitching takes longer to rip than it does to sew, and this could turn into a very time-consuming project if you make a mistake. But before I tell you how to sew, you'll need to pin the layers together.

### Pinning the fabric for sewing

Initially, until the face is completely sewn, you will be working on a three-layer sandwich. Set aside the square of fabric with the iron-on facing for later use. Lay down the fabric square that has no markings. Place the double layer of batting on top of it, and lay the square with the entire face tracing on top of it all. The face should be clearly visible to you, with the wrong side of the fabric turned in to the batting. Secure a few pins in each corner to hold it all together before you begin stitching.

### The stitch

You want to cover all of your lines with thread, and I've found a back running stitch to be the best way to do this. (See Stitch Glossary.) If you're an accomplished embroiderer, you can apply your skill in that craft to your soft sculpture. You can use a chain stitch around the outlines of the nose, and a satin stitch for the lips. But if you don't have much experience with hand sewing, or if you want a simple, folksy look to your face, I suggest the back running stitch. It will look like a very small running stitch, but have the strength of a backstitch.

Start sewing the features, not the outline. Be certain to sew through all three layers and to begin at the chin and work your way up. Also, pull the stitches tight. Your goal is to achieve a sculpted look, and the stitching is actually redistributing the batting. If you notice the fabric puckering a bit, all the better. It's doing what it's supposed to do, and each pucker adds character to the finished face.

### The thread

Although you can sew in a color that contrasts with your fabric, to emphasize the lines of the features, I prefer to stitch in white. The white stitching on the white canvas gives the face a natural, more subtle character. Generally, I prefer to match my thread to my fabric for any sort of top-stitching, but that is nothing more than a personal preference.

### Hints on sewing the face

As I said earlier, begin sewing with the chin. I have a cleft in the diagram. Sew it first. Then sew the lines of the mouth and the wrinkles between the nose and the mouth. The nose is the hardest feature to get right and will require some stuffing and poking.

### The nose

Sew along the outside of the nose, but not across the bridge. Pull off a few small pieces of batting (about the size of the cotton at the end of a Q-tip) and roll them into small balls. From the top of the face, insert this extra stuffing between the batting and the top layer of fabric and push it down into the nose with your probe instrument (a chopstick, the handle of a paintbrush, etc.). Keep pushing that stuffing in until the nose is slightly more raised than any of the other features. A good nose gives character to a face. Later, when we make the face vase (page 94), we'll carry that concept to its extreme.

When you think your face has an adequately stuffed nose, sew across the bridge. This final stitching will keep all the stuffing in place.

This process of poking extra bits of stuffing to form special shapes is really the meat of soft sculpture. On a project like this you are indeed a sculptor. If you were working in clay you'd be adding bits of that clay to define shape. If you were working in marble you'd have to chisel away excess material. In this medium you regulate shape by adding or decreasing the stuffing.

### Finishing the hand stitching

When you have sewn all the features in place, sew around the oval outline of the face. Again, start sewing at the chin. If you think the cheeks should be fuller, poke a bit of extra stuffing into them, just as you did with the nose, and continue sewing. This extra stuffing is not really necessary to make a good face, but it's fun to poke around with your creation, and you may achieve some interesting, individualized results.

### Sewing on the back

Your face is finished and you're ready to add the finishing touches. Lay the square of fabric with the iron-on facing over your soft face, with the iron-on facing and the oval outline up and the right side of the fabric down. Pin around the edge of the square and put it into machine, iron-on facing up. (See illustration 25).

Set your machine for 12 stitches per inch, and use the oval line as a sewing line.

Begin sewing where an ear might be, continue down around the chin, and end where the other ear would be. (My faces have no ears, so as to hear no evil.)

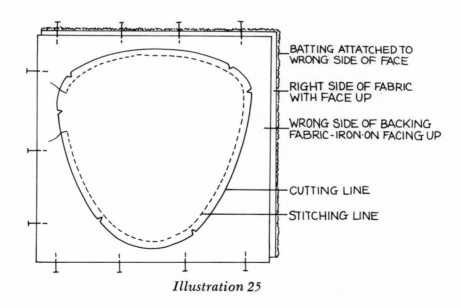

BATTING ATTATCHED TO WRONG SIDE OF FACE

RIGHT SIDE OF FABRIC WITH FACE UP

WRONG SIDE OF BACKING FABRIC-IRON-ON FACING UP

CUTTING LINE

STITCHING LINE

*Illustration 25*

### Turning out a face

When you have finished stitching around the face—double stitching the beginning and end of your line—take it out of the machine, put your thumbs in the unsewn pocket, and turn the buckle inside out.

Everything should look fine and finished and bald.

## FINISHING

### The hair

There are a dozen ways you can give your face a good head of hair. The easiest, I suppose, would be to draw it on with a felt-tip pen. The result will be a bit flat-looking, but there are times when that's exactly the look you want. An alternative is to make hair out of wool or embroidery thread. Again, the embroidery thread will have a flatter look that may work very well with your face. You can coif your face with a smooth satin stitch. Just draw the outline for the hairline and fill it in with stitches.

If you use wool, as I did, there are still several variations. Begin by closing the top of the head with the hidden running stitch. (See Stitch Glossary.) Thread a wool needle with the wool. Don't make a knot at the end; as you sew, the thread will secure itself, just as it does in needlepoint. Make small stitches, not in any predictable order, and *don't* pull the thread tight. In fact, leave a good-sized loop of wool with each stitch, and put the needle back into the head very close to the place you pulled it out from.

When you sew the hair this way, make certain to take only one layer of fabric in with each stitch. You should not put the needle in the front of the head and pull it out the back. Keep stitching loops all over the top of the head, around the face, and around just a bit of the back. No one will see the back, and the buckle will lie flatter if you don't add any bulk to its back.

Another kind of hair you can make with wool involves the machine. Hold your hand out straight with your thumb outstretched and the other four fingers pressed together. Wrap your four fingers with wool—not too tightly—about fifteen times. If you want your face to have thicker hair, wrap the wool a few more turns.

Slip the wool off your fingers and insert one of the folded ends of it into the unfinished pocket at the top of your face. Put a few pins in to secure the front of the face to the back and make sure to distribute the wool evenly between the two. Then stitch, very close to the edge, through all three layers. Double stitch the beginning and end of the line.

Insert the tip of your scissors through the many loops of wool you just attached and snip, forming single strands of wool. If you pull some of it forward and cut it just above the eyes, you can shape bangs or whatever kind of coiffure you want.

You may have to stitch a bit of it down, to give it direction, but there should be enough wool to cover any stitches.

### Applying makeup

Your face is finished but pale. It probably could use a bit of color in its cheeks, perhaps a bit of red on the lips, and maybe even some eye shadow. The extent to which you color your face is entirely up to you. It's the easiest and most whimsical part of the project. It's no more difficult than using a coloring book. Just use different-colored felt-tipped pens, and fill in the spaces between the stitching. I suggest you use some color on the eyes, and fill the pupils in entirely. This type of eye treatment will give the face some focus.

Look at the picture of my buckle for some ideas and then let yourself go!

## THE BELT

You can attach your face buckle to almost any kind of belt, but I've found the following method particularly effective.

Measure your waist and cut a piece of heavyweight macramé cord to a length of double your measurement plus six inches. (If you want to wear the belt around your hips, cut the cord to double your hip measurement plus six inches.

Fold the cord in half and tie a knot a few inches from the folded end and another knot at each loose end of the cord. Tie the two knotted ends together with a third knot. (See illustration 17.) This procedure is exactly the same as for the white cord of the rainbow pendant.

Now attach the cord to your buckle with a simple overstitch (see Stitch Glossary), as indicated in illustration 26.

The knot at the folded end of the cord will serve as a loop, and the three knots at the other end of the cord will form a button.

This simple length of macramé cord serves very well as a belt for your fabric buckle. If, however, you really know your macramé knotting, you might consider knotting an entire belt and then stitching it onto your buckle. You can always use a loop and button as a fastener.

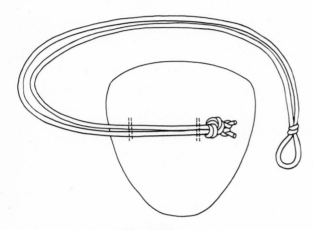

*Illustration 26*

# Fern Pillow

While there's clearly no question that the plant came before the pillow, there's no getting around the fact that the pillow goes back a long, long way. And, as Jerry said in his preface, the pillow is really the great-great-grandmother of soft sculpture.

Since I live in an apartment in the middle of New York City, I don't get the opportunity to see all of the trees that I'd like to. My body's requirement for "seeing green" is very rarely met. In an effort to combat my deprivation, I decided to make an all-out effort with house plants, and the windows in my living room are filled with vines, trees, cacti, and all kinds of strange plants. But my effort to bring the life on my windowsills into some dark corners of the living room was frustrating, and after a long time spent watching healthy plants turn yellow and die, I hit on the idea of the fern pillow. The fern pillow you're about to make is an elaborate variation on the ordinary pillow, but it suited my particular needs, and may be the answer to a decorating problem of yours as well. It successfully achieves the illusion I was aiming for, but goes one step further—in the direction of elegance—than the real thing might have.

Since I wanted my finished product to be imitative of a real plant, I chose to do the leaves in green satin. The green was an obvious choice, and the sheen of the satin acted as an exaggeration of the waxy leaf surface. The very broad selection of green satins I found when I got to the fabric store confused me at first. I couldn't decide between a muted forest green and a very bright emerald green. Ultimately I chose both, using the muted color for the underside of each leaf and the brighter color for the top, although I suggest that you use the same color for top and

bottom the first time you make this pattern. Ideas often come to me when I'm in the fabric store, surrounded by all the possibilities. It's important to go in knowing what you want, but good to keep your mind open to any possibility suggested by your surroundings.

For the base of my pillow I had wanted a nubby brown cotton. Again, I thought that would work well as an imitation of nature. I didn't see exactly what I wanted, but found instead a brown brushed denim. It wasn't very far off my original target and worked well with the satin. After looking at many fabrics I still felt drawn to it, and decided to trust my instincts. The denim has a soft feeling and adds a touch of whimsy to a rather serious, formal pillow.

I'm still curious about how a nubbier base would look, and may someday make a similar pillow with just such a fabric. But I enjoy the mixture of abstraction and realism my fern pillow encompasses. You may, of course, choose to make a different mix. I've also entertained the thought of doing the leaves in a striped polished cotton. Polished cotton is less formal than satin, it has a sheen, and it would be suitable for the kitchen table, hanging in a dim window, or just dropped on a bed. The choice of fabric here, as in all of the projects, is up to you. Think about where you want the pillow, and the kind of effect for which you're aiming. If you want it to blend harmoniously with a room, then make that your priority; forget about verisimilitude and use whatever the room calls for. If you want to create a bit of *trompe l'oeil*, then think more in terms of making the pillow look as close to the real thing as you can. And if you're very adventurous, don't make any decision until you're in the fabric store and actually faced with all the possibilities.

## WHAT YOU WILL NEED

- 2½ yards fabric
- 1¼ yards iron-on facing
- 100% polyester thread to match fabric
- ½ yard fabric for base
- ¼ yard iron-on facing for base (optional)
- roll of polyester batting
- 3 pounds cow peas (or any dry bean)
- plenty of pins and small needle
- probe tool (chopstick, paintbrush, etc.)
- salad plate
- sharp scissors
- felt-tip pen
- cardboard or oak tag

## MAKING THE PATTERN

The pattern for the fern pillow is so easy you could sketch it all freehand, but I'd suggest following these guidelines.

### Base

For the base, use a salad plate as your guide. The size is right to accommodate ten or more leaves, and when you fill it with beans it will flop nicely over the arm of a chair.

Trace the perimeter of the salad plate on the oak tag, cut it out, and put this circular template aside until later.

### Leaves

You will be making a total of ten leaves. (You can make more or less, as you wish, but I've found that ten leaves make a good, full pillow.) The leaves should be made in three sizes, as follows: two of the largest leaves; four medium-size leaves; and four of the smallest leaves. (See the chart that follows for size.)

Begin by drawing three crosses, like the one in illustration 27, directly on your oak tag according to the dimensions specified in the chart.

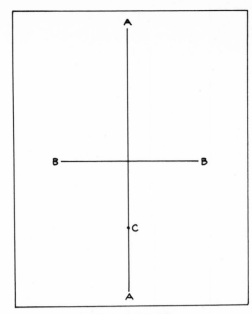

*Illustration 27*

When you have made each of the three crosses, you are ready to draw your leaves. Before you draw the leaves, however, check the dimensions of your crosses. Line B should always be half the size of line A. Point C is always halfway between the bottom of line A and line B.

| Leaf | Line A | Line B | Point C |
|---|---|---|---|
| Big | 16″ | 8″ | 4″ and up |
| Medium | 13″ | 6½″ | 3¼″ and up |
| Small | 10″ | 5″ | 2½″ and up |

The next step in making your pattern requires a touch of artistic skill, but if you can connect the dots in a child's coloring book, you shouldn't have any problem with it. You simply trace the outline of a leaf around the cross you've just drawn. The point of the leaf should be at the top of line A. It should widen to accommodate line B, and taper into a stem beginning at point C. (See illustration 28.)

When you've drawn one of each size leaf on the oak tag, cut them out and put them with the template for the base.

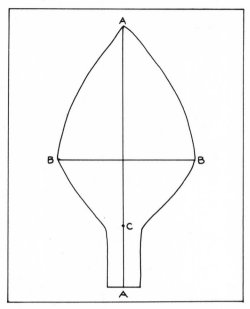

*Illustration 28*

## CUTTING

You will be cutting through double layers of fabric, so make certain your scissors are sharp and you're cutting on a smooth, hard surface.

### *Laying out and cutting the satin leaves*

If the top and bottom of your leaf are the same fabric, simply double the fabric, right sides facing in, and pin along the edge. If you decide to use two different fabrics on each leaf, lay them together, right sides facing in, and pin along two opposite sides.

Now place the oak-tag template for the largest leaf at the edge of the doubled fabric and draw around its perimeter with a pencil or a ballpoint pen. Don't ever draw on satin with a felt-tip pen, because the fabric will absorb the ink and your line will bleed. When you have traced around the entire template, move the oak tag over and trace a second leaf. Put the large-size-leaf template aside and trace around the medium-size leaf four times. When you have

finished tracing around the perimeter of the medium leaf, repeat the same procedure with the smallest leaf.

You should have the outlines of ten leaves on your fabric. Place a few pins inside each leaf and cut through the doubled fabric around the lines you have just drawn. Put the leaves aside.

### *Laying out and cutting the iron-on facing*

Now lay out your iron-on facing, single thickness, on a smooth, hard surface. Trace all ten leaves onto the facing, just as you did previously on the fabric. When you have them all drawn, cut them out carefully and put them aside.

## BATTING

In this particular pattern it is wise to use polyester batting, rather than a loose stuffing. (See "Stuffings.") The finished leaf should be smooth and even, with no irregularities or bulges, and batting insures this kind of smooth finish.

### *Ironing the facing onto the batting*

Unroll your batting over an ironing board, letting the excess drape over each side. Batting comes in different thicknesses, and you have to decide how thick you want each leaf to be. I always like things with more stuffing rather than less, so I double the batting. Simply fold the batting to form a double thickness.

Apply the iron-on-facing leaves to the batting, one by one. Read the instructions that come with your iron-on facing and follow them carefully. Generally, the iron should be dry, set for cotton, and left over the facing for five seconds. When you have attached all ten of the iron-on-facing leaves to the batting, cut them out. For the sake of clarity, we'll refer to these leaves with attached batting as "faced leaves" from now on.

Making these faced leaves is very important. It simplifies the sewing because it gives a firm definition to the batting, and it adds body to your final leaf. You'll find, as you work, that iron-on facing is often a good idea, even if you use it just to reinforce fabric.

Now you should have two piles: one of faced leaves; the other of satin leaves.

You are ready to sew!

## SEWING

As you've seen, there's a great deal of work in making a soft sculpture besides sewing. If you've gotten this far with me, the rest should be a breeze.

### Pinning the fabric leaves onto the faced leaves

Place the faced leaves, iron-on-facing side down, on the floor. Now you have to match the fabric leaves to the faced ones. Remember, there are three different-size leaves, and you have cut two pieces of fabric (a top and a bottom) for each leaf. Lay one fabric leaf, right side up, over each faced leaf. Lay the matching piece of fabric over the first, but this piece must be placed wrong side up. The end result of this laying of fabrics should be ten three-layered leaves. Pin the layers of fabric and faced leaves together, but don't pierce the facing with the pins. If you try to catch all of the batting and facing in the pin, you'll find that the fabric will gather, and you will not be able to sew smoothly. All you really need to catch in each pin is the double-layered fabric and a bit of the soft batting. It may not feel like it's holding, but it has a strong enough grip to be run through the machine. As always, place your pins perpendicular to the seam.

An alternative to all this pinning is loose basting. Basting works well, but is somewhat more time-consuming than pinning. If you baste the fabric to the batting, run the needle through the iron-on facing as well as the batting, and don't pull the thread tightly.

### Drawing the seam line

You are nearly ready to sew, but again you are faced with several alternatives. If you want to have a straight-edged leaf, use a ballpoint pen or a pencil and draw a guideline on the top layer of fabric. Remember, this should be the wrong side of the fabric so nothing will show in your final product. I suggest you use 1/4" seams, so follow the outer shape of the leaf with your pen approximately 1/4" in from the edge.

Rather than straight-seam my leaves, I chose to scallop the edges. This involves a good deal more work and dexterity, but it adds a very nice touch. Again, you must draw a guideline on the top layer of fabric, but the line you draw will have to conform to the scallop shape you choose. (See illustration 29.)

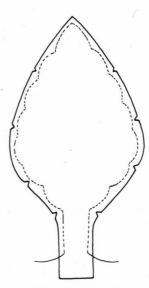

*Illustration 29*

### Placing the leaf in the machine

As always, before you put the actual project in your machine, pin together a piece of scrap batting and two pieces of fabric to use as a stitch and tension test. I've been most successful sewing these leaves with 12 stitches to an inch on my seams, and a thread tension of about 6. But machines are quirky, and you probably know best how to handle yours.

Now place your leaf into the machine with the fabric facing up and the iron-on facing on the bottom. The seam line you've drawn should be clearly visible. Put the needle in the line about an inch up from the bottom of the leaf and sew—carefully following your hand-drawn guideline—around the side, the leaf tip, and back up the opposite side until you reach a point just horizontal to where you began.

Make certain to double stitch the beginning and end of your seam for reinforcement. Take the leaf out of the machine when you've finished sewing and turn it over. Hopefully, you'll see a stitched duplicate of your seam guideline showing through the facing. Once the line is sewn, the leaf is ready to be turned.

Repeat this stitching process on each of your leaves.

### Turning out a leaf

The crucial trick of making things with batting revolves around assemblage. The manner in which we've placed the fabrics makes it possible to turn the whole leaf right side out and end up with a remarkably smooth finish. It would be very difficult to achieve this kind of effect if you were stuffing with some kind of loose fiberfill.

By now you have had a great deal of practice at turning projects right side out. The procedure is always the same. It might be helpful to you, at this point, to refer back to some of the earlier projects to refresh your memory.

You will be turning the project out through the hole at the base of the stem, and the finished leaf should have satin on top and on bottom, with a double layer of batting in between.

When your leaf has emerged right side out through the unsewn bottom of the stem, you'll probably find that it still does not look anything like the precise shape you sewed a few minutes ago. Most likely, the tip is barely showing, and all of the details of your scalloped edge are lost. The reason it looks lumpy and misshapen is that most of it is still in hiding, and needs a few pokes to come out.

Insert your tool through the opening and run it along the seam line. Don't be timid about this step. Your seams are strong and will withhold a good poke. Push out the tip and follow the seam

line until it looks exactly as you planned. Only when you are completely satisfied with the shape of your leaf will you know that you're finished pushing and poking.

### Finishing the stem

Everything on your leaf should look neat and clean now, with the exception of the stem. The stem is still unfinished and probably is showing all sorts of loose threads and excess batting. To finish the leaf we have to close the stem to conform with the other seams.

Fold the raw edge of the fabric on both sides of the stem approximately 1/4". You can use your seam line as a guide. Sew the hole closed with a small overstitch. (See Stitch Glossary.) This is the same method of closing an opening on the seam line that you have used throughout the book.

Finally you have what looks like a finished leaf. It should be shaped just as you drew it; it should be evenly stuffed and plump-looking. It should, in fact, be everything you ever wanted in a stuffed leaf . . . almost.

### Top-stitching

Again you are faced with a choice. You can call your leaf finished and begin to make the base, or you can add one more finishing touch— the top-stitching—in the interest of verisimilitude. I always have trouble letting go of a project, and usually add extra finishing touches. Top-stitching doesn't require a lot of work. With a bit of practice, it's easy and quick. And it gives the leaf a nice tailored look. I suggest that you look at the photograph of my finished project to get a clear picture of what top-stitching on the leaves looks like, and if you decide to include it, refer to illustration 30.

On your first leaf, use a piece of tailor's chalk and draw a line straight down the middle. This line represents the main vein of the leaf. Put the leaf in the machine, readjust your stitch setting to 8 stitches per inch, and sew along the line. Reinforce the bottom and top of the line by double stitching. When you remove the leaf from the machine, snip the excess thread as close to the fabric as you can get.

This middle seam may be all the top-stitching you want, in which case you need only repeat the process on the other ten leaves. I get a bit carried away with myself and have added a few additional arteries. (See illustration 30.) These additional lines can be drawn in whatever shape or quantity you choose. You'll find that if you add too many (as I did on my first leaf) the batting will bunch up and you will be sacrificing softness for veins! So keep the top-stitching down to four or five lines.

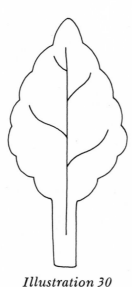

*Illustration 30*

You may also want to experiment with a contrasting color on your top-stitching. If the leaf is green, you may try top-stitching with yellow thread. I was most pleased with stitching in the same color thread I used on my seams. The effect is more subtle, and to me more pleasing.

Finally you can hold up your leaf and feel content. So far as I can tell, it is finished. You may, of course, want to do any number of other things to it. If something occurs to you, please go ahead and experiment. The worst that can happen is that you may lose a leaf. I lose leaves on my real plants all the time, and as a rule they

look none the worse for the loss. The advantage of losing a leaf on a soft pillow, as opposed to a real plant, is that you can always stitch up a replacement. It's almost always worth the gamble to experiment with your ideas.

## THE BASE

I chose to stuff the base with beans because their weight enabled me to balance my pillow just about anywhere. The beanbag base can sit unprecariously on the arm of a sofa or chair, and the leaves can fall in whatever direction they choose. If I had stuffed the base with something as lightweight as the batting, the top and bottom of my pillow would have been fighting each other. And if I had stuffed the leaves with anything as heavy as beans, they would have drooped. Remember, if you want something to be stable, the bottom must be heavier than the top.

### Cutting the fabric

It's time to find the circular oak-tag template you made for the base. Lay out the brown brushed denim and fold it with right sides together. Place the circular template over the doubled fabric and trace around the perimeter of your pattern with a felt-tip pen.

When the outline of the circle is clearly drawn, put a few pins through both layers of fabric, inside the line. Cut carefully along the line.

Keep the two circles pinned together, exactly as they are right now, but arrange the pins more carefully around the edge, so that they are all pointing toward the center of the circle.

### Reinforcement

If you selected a lightweight fabric for your base, I suggest that you reinforce it with iron-on facing before you stuff it. Simply use your salad plate again and trace its perimeter on your facing. Cut it out and, following the instructions on the package, iron it onto your fabric.

*Illustration 31*

### Putting the base into the machine and sewing

Set your stitch gauge on 12 stitches per inch and put the pinned base into your machine. Put the needle in the fabric and lower the presser foot so that it falls on the outer edge of the circle. You will be using the presser foot, as you have in other projects, as a guide to insure a 1/4″ seam line. Sew carefully around the edge of the circle. Allow approximately a 2″ hold for stuffing.

Turn the round base inside out.

### Stuffing

I used cow peas for my stuffing because they were the cheapest beans on the supermarket shelf. There is no need to be extravagant in this area. Save your money for some special fabric.

Insert the narrow end of a kitchen funnel in the small opening you left for stuffing, and start filling it with beans. The funnel may get congested from time to time, but if you shake it a bit, or stick your probe tool through it, it will clear up. Once you have filled the bag with approximately two pounds of beans you can stop. The bag must not be too full or it won't balance properly on an armchair.

### Finishing the base

Now finish the base just as you finished the stem on the leaves. Fold the raw edge of the fabric in 1/4″ to conform with the seam line and stitch it closed with a small overstitch. (See Stitch Glossary.)

## ATTACHING THE LEAVES TO THE BASE

There are any number of ways to attach the leaves to the base of your pillow. If you want to be able to change the position of your leaves with any regularity, you can attach them to the base with snaps or Velcro. This method of attaching the leaves doesn't seem necessary for a formal pillow. If, however, you are making the pillow from cotton, as a child's toy, it might be fun to have the leaves "arrangeable."

I suggest that you sew the leaves directly onto the base.

### Placing the leaves

Look at illustration 31 for placement of the leaves. I have arranged them in three concentric circles on the top of the base. The circles are similar to three paths of orbit. Place the two largest leaves opposite each other on the perimeter of the largest circle.

The four middle-size leaves fit, as indicated in illustration 31, at even intervals along the middle circle.

Finally, the four smallest leaves fit at even intervals along the smallest circle.

Setting the leaves according to this plan allows each leaf to fall either forward or backward without covering another leaf. This placement also gives the pillow a very full effect.

### Sewing the leaves to the base

Pin the leaf where you want it and sew, with a small overstitch (see Stitch Glossary), up either side of the stem. I suggest you sew up only one half the length of the stem on each side, to allow maximum flexibility.

## THE COMPLETED PILLOW

Once the leaves are all attached to the base, your pillow is complete. Throw it on your couch, a chair arm, your bed, or make a coil pot (directions are given later) to put it in. I suggest first putting it on top of the pillow on your bed, laying your head down, closing your eyes, and taking a little nap. This was a complicated project and you've earned yourself a rest!

# Heart Evening Bag

## A Jerry Kott Design

There's something very appealing and versatile about hearts. Think of how they're used in folk art: printed on the side of a barn in Pennsylvania Dutch country, cut into a window shutter on a chalet in Switzerland. The landlord of our cabin this summer had stenciled a bright red heart onto the screen door, and, as silly as it seemed at first, we grew to like it. Contrast these applications of the heart shape with the tiny, delicate gold pendant you may be wearing around your neck. And contrast the pendant with a heart-shaped box of chocolates. They're all the same shape, but they say different things. Shapes are never trite—it's what you do with them that counts.

Jerry's use of this shape made me rethink its potential. The combination of the folksy heart shape and the sophistication and elegance of a satin evening bag makes this project as outstanding as all of Jerry's original designs.

Jerry's first soft sculpture, nearly fifteen years ago, was a heart, and he's still finding exciting ways to deal with the same shape. He has designed the bag in satin—a flashy, formal, evening fabric—with some very clean, unfussy linear quilting. The bag is just large enough to accommodate a comb, compact, and lipstick—just enough for a formal gathering—and Jerry specifically suggests that you don't enlarge it. You may end up with a bag that holds a great deal more, but does so with less charm. Everything about his design, right down to the length of the shoulder strap, works just so.

You can, of course, vary the color of your satin. I've seen the bag made up in black, in red, and in gold lamé—all of which work well. I particularly like the idea of making it into a bride's bag, from white satin, perhaps as a shower gift. Or you can make it in a color that will complement or match your gown.

The shoulder strap is heavy-gauge silk macramé cord, and should match the fabric of the bag in color. This type of cording is available in a wide variety of colors, so matching your fabric shouldn't be difficult.

The quilting, like the cord, should be done in the same color thread as your fabric. There are times, of course, when I recommend contrasting-color quilting, but this isn't one of them. Since the key to the bag is understatement, fussing it up with a lot of colors would only interfere. Even the lines of the quilting are simple.

Although the bag is not difficult to make, it can be a bit awkward to handle while you're making it, which is why we didn't include it among the first few projects of the book. But don't be intimidated by it. If you've worked your way up to this point, it won't pose any problems, and you'll be delighted with the results.

### SPINNING OFF

As I said, the heart bag is so perfectly proportioned and designed that I don't really recommend tampering with it. But Jerry is a bit less religious about his designs than I, and he's offered a few suggestions. First, there is the possibility of not quilting. The method and pattern are the same whether you quilt or not, so you needn't alter your procedure. The best reason *not* to quilt is a change in fabric. If you decide, for example, to use a velour rather than satin, the bag would look better unquilted. And the bag certainly would be beautiful in velour.

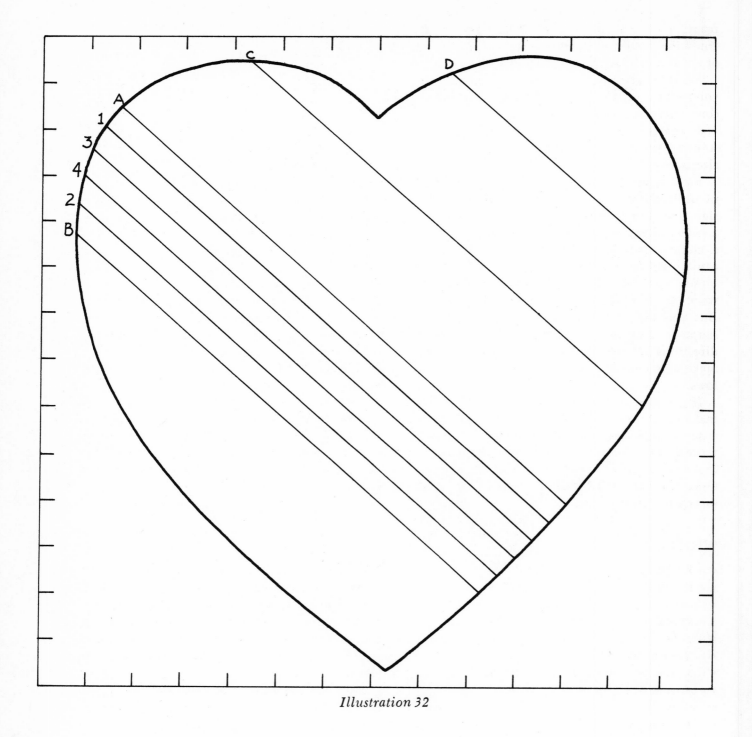

*Illustration 32*

You might also consider embroidering the front of the heart bag instead of quilting. If you know some crewel stitches, the combination of crafts would be particularly effective here.

Another alteration that Jerry suggests involves the strap. Rather than using a matching cord, there are hundreds of possibilities in ribbons that would make interesting and delicate straps. Lace might also work as an interesting alternative.

Finally, you may decide to do a different kind of quilting, rather than use Jerry's linear design. He once made this bag for his niece with a swan quilted on it. You can make your initials, a circle—virtually anything you can sew, you can quilt.

As I said earlier, I don't think this bag will work well if you make it larger or less formal. But you can do other things with the heart shape by altering its size. If you use the grid directions in "How to Use This Book," you can make small heart pendants or large heart pillows.

If you care to be a bit adventurous, you can make the same sort of bag in a shape other than a heart. The procedure is the same, and if you want to use a denim, or cotton, you can make it look like a piece of fruit, or even an animal. Once you begin so major an alteration as that, there's no limit on size.

## WHAT YOU WILL NEED

- 5″ thin silk macramé cord
- 42″ heavy macramé cord
- 16″ × 9″ iron-on interfacing (woven or non-woven)
- ¼ yard dacron batting
- ¼ yard rayon satin
- polyester thread to match fabric
- satin pins
- a tiny button
- sewing-tracing paper
- carbon paper
- typing paper
- cardboard or oak tag

## MAKING THE PATTERN

Lay a regular piece of typing paper over the tracing page (illustration 32) and trace the entire heart design, including quilting lines. Now lay the typing paper, with the design transfer, over a piece of cardboard and slip the carbon paper between the two. (See illustration 2 in "How to Use This Book.") With a ballpoint pen, trace over the outside line of the heart. Put the typing paper aside for later use and cut out the cardboard heart template.

## CUTTING THE FABRIC

### The satin

Lay the satin face up on a hard, flat surface and with a ballpoint pen trace a row of four hearts directly onto the fabric, carefully following the edge of the cardboard pattern. Do not cut on a bias. Once you have outlined all four hearts, cut them out.

### The interfacing

Lay your iron-on interfacing on a hard, flat surface, glued side down, and, using your cardboard template and a ballpoint pen, trace two hearts on it. Cut out the hearts.

## ATTACHING THE FACING

Unroll the dacron batting and drape it over an ironing board. Place the hearts you have just cut from the iron-on facing over the batting, glued side down, and follow the manufacturer's instructions for attaching. It is generally suggested to use a dry iron on a cotton setting for 15 seconds.

After you have attached the facing to the dacron batting, follow the shape of the iron-on interfacing and cut out two hearts.

At this point you will have four satin hearts and two batting hearts, with iron-on interfacing attached to one side.

## TRANSFERRING THE QUILTING LINES TO THE SATIN

Take a satin heart and lay it face up on a hard surface. Lay the typing paper (with the quilting lines) over the satin, and carefully pin them together at the upper dip and lower tip of the heart. Keep your pins as close to the edge as possible.

Now slip a piece of seamstress tracing paper (as close in color to your fabric as possible) in between the two pinned pieces. (See illustration 3.) Make certain that the shiny side of the tracing paper is facing the shiny side of the satin.

With a straight edge and a sharp pencil, go over the quilting lines on the typing paper. This procedure will transfer the quilting lines to the face of the fabric.

Repeat this procedure on a second satin heart.

### Pinning for quilting

In this step you will be using only four pieces: the two batting hearts and the two satin hearts you have just transferred the quilting lines to.

Pin a batting heart to a marked satin heart as follows: Lay the batting on a table with the iron-on-facing side down, the loose fluffy side up. Over the loose side of the batting, place the wrong side of your satin heart—making sure to align the edges carefully. The shiny side of the satin, with all the quilting lines, should be facing you.

I suggest that you put your first pin at the bottom tip of the heart, and your second pin at the point of cleavage on the top. When both of these pins are securely placed, pin at even intervals, close to the edge, around the entire perimeter of the heart.

Repeat this procedure with the second batting heart and marked satin heart.

## QUILTING

The quilting process is really quite simple, and, as you'll see, it is much more difficult to explain than it is to do. To simplify the process, I have arranged the text directly below each illustration. As you read the text, keep checking the illustrations.

Before you begin the quilting look over illustrations 33–39. In each case the broken line indicates where you will be stitching. This line has arrows on it that indicate the direction of your stitching. The solid line indicates what you have already sewn. As always, practice on scraps before you touch the real thing. When you feel you have adjusted the tension and pressure on your machine (a medium setting is usually best), and the tension inside your head, to a comfortable setting, you are ready to begin working on the bag.

### Inserting the bag into the machine

Place your pinned satin-and-batting heart into the machine, satin side up, so that the needle is just above point A. It's important to keep the shiny side of the satin up, lest it catch on the teeth of your sewing machine and snag.

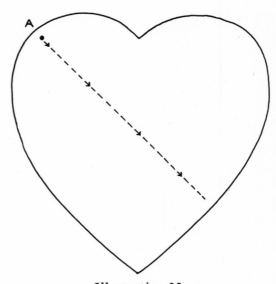

*Illustration 33*

Insert the needle at point A and sew down line A. Remove the bag from the machine.

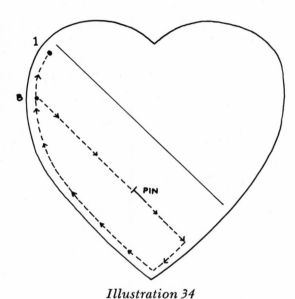

*Illustration 34*

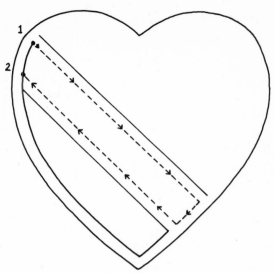

*Illustration 35*

Turn the heart as I describe above and sew down point 1. Turn the heart again and sew as indicated along the edge of the heart and up line 2. Again, leave the needle in the heart.

Insert the needle at point B and sew down line B. (Jerry found that the fabric tended to slip when he sewed line B, but he solved the problem by inserting a pin in the direction of the line). At the end of the line, leave the needle in your fabric, lift the presser foot, and turn the heart so that you will be in the right position to sew down toward the point of the heart. (This type of turning insures a sharp corner.) Lower the presser foot and sew counterclockwise around the bottom of the heart and back up one side, to point 1. Leave the heart in the machine.

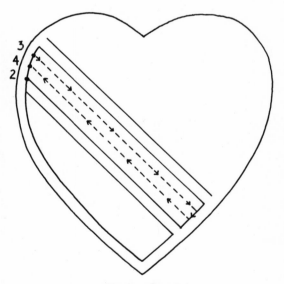

*Illustration 36*

Resew, as indicated, from point 2 to point 3, turn the heart, and sew down line 3. At the bottom of line 3, turn the heart again, sew just a bit along the perimeter, and sew up line 4. Remove the heart from the machine.

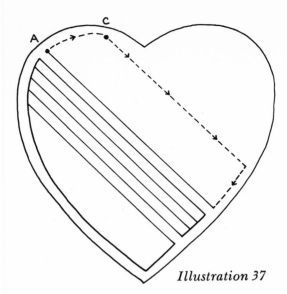

*Illustration 37*

Insert the heart into your machine with the needle at point A. Sew as indicated in a clockwise direction to point C, and down line C. Turn the heart and stitch from the end of line C to the end of line A. Remove the heart from the machine.

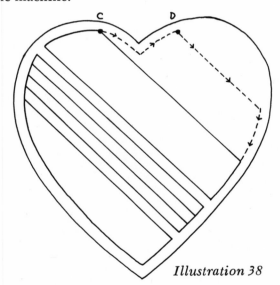

*Illustration 38*

Insert the heart into the machine with the needle at point C. Sew carefully as indicated along the dip of the heart to point D, and turn the heart as you have been doing. Sew down line D, turn the heart again, and sew down the edge of the heart to the end of line C. Remove the heart from the machine.

*Illustration 39*

Insert the heart at point D and sew as indicated in a clockwise direction, over the hump of the heart to the end of line D.

## ATTACHING THE LOOP

Take the 5″ thin silk cord and tie knots ¼″ in from each end. (See illustration 40.) Lay one of the quilted hearts, satin face up, over illustration 40. Mark the placement of the loop—point B and point C—as indicated. Keep the marks close to the edge of the fabric, and baste the loop in place along the seam line, approximately ½″ in from the knotted ends. Be sure to look carefully at illustration 40 for placement of the loop. The knots should be facing up, and the actual loop should face the point of the heart.

## SEWING QUILTED HEARTS TOGETHER

Hold one of the quilted hearts directly over illustration 40 and on the batting mark point A and point D with a ballpoint pen. Keep these marks close to the edge of the heart.

Repeat this step on the second quilted heart. Now lay the quilted hearts together so that

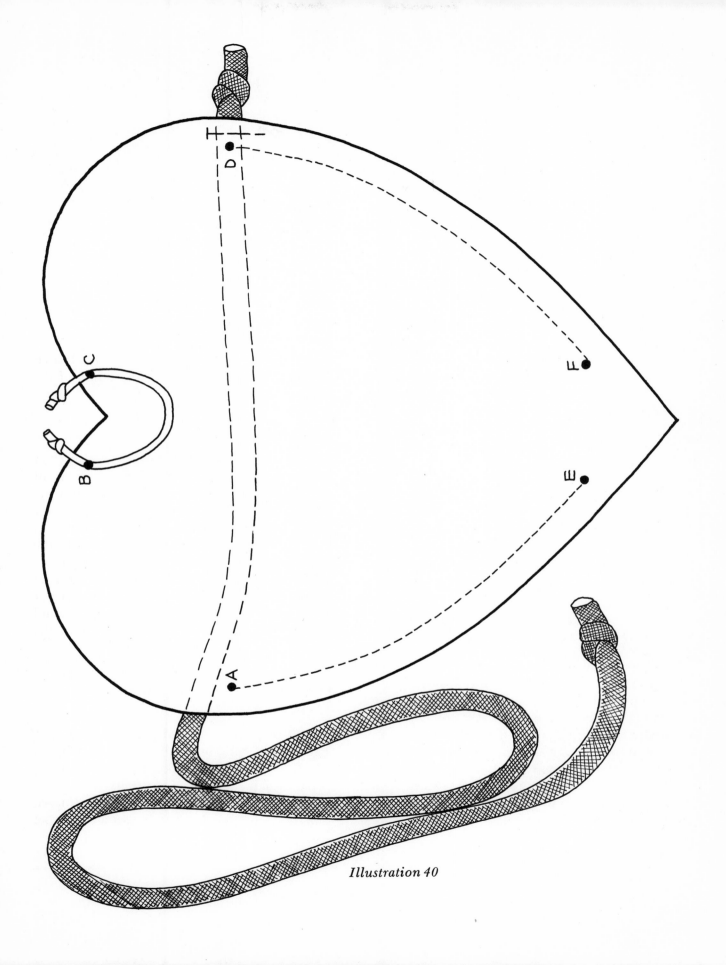

*Illustration 40*

the right sides are facing in. Place one pin at the bottom tip of the heart, a second at the top dip, and continue to pin the two quilted pieces together, inserting the pins at even intervals along the edge.

Insert the hearts into your sewing machine, allowing approximately ½″ for seam allowance, and sew from point A around the bottom of the heart counterclockwise and back up to point D. Put aside.

## SEWING THE LINING

It's time to find those other two pieces of unquilted satin heart that you put aside at the beginning of this project. These two pieces, unbatted and unquilted, will be the lining of your finished bag.

As you did with the quilted hearts, hold a satin heart, wrong side up, over illustration 40 and mark points A, B, C, and D with a ballpoint pen, close to the fabric's edge. Repeat the same procedure with the second satin heart.

Now pin these two lining hearts together, right sides facing in.

## PREPARING THE SHOULDER STRAP

Take the long, heavy macramé cord (which will serve as your shoulder strap) and tie a knot ¼″ in from each end. Look carefully at illustration 40 and lay the cord, as indicated, across line AD, inside the pocket formed by the two lining hearts. Insert a pin at point D.

Put the lining pocket into the machine with the needle at point A. (See illustration 40.) Make certain not to go through the macramé cord with the needle. You must take care not to sew through the cord on this side of the bag. Sew, as indicated in illustration 40, down to point E, with ½″ seam allowance. Remove the lining from your machine and reinsert it with the needle at point F. Sew up the edge of the heart from point F to point D (see illustration 40), this time making certain to sew through the cord. Remove.

## ATTACHING THE LINING TO THE QUILTING

This is the trickiest step of the project, and it will be easiest to explain if we look first at what we have and label everything carefully.

At this point you should have two heart-shaped pockets—a quilted one and an unquilted one—each with the wrong side facing out.

Each of these pockets has four rounded humps at the top of it. For the sake of clarity, take a ballpoint pen and lable the four humps on the quilted pocket consecutively A, B, C, and D. (See illustration 41.) Make your markings small and close to the edge, on the iron-on facing. Put this quilted heart-pocket aside for a moment.

Now take the unquilted satin heart-pocket and, on the wrong side of the fabric, mark the humps consecutively a, b, c, and d. (See illustration 41.) Again, make your markings close to the edge of the fabric.

Now comes the awkward step. We are going to attach the quilted heart-pocket to the lining heart-pocket by sewing hump A to hump a, hump B to hump b, hump C to hump c, and hump D to hump d. Look first at illustration 41 and then at illustration 42 to see the process before you actually do it. You'll note from illustration 42 that when you pin the humps of the quilted hearts to the corresponding humps on the unquilted hearts, you should be pinning the right sides of the fabric together.

What you have now looks nothing at all like an evening bag. In fact, if you stuffed this pinned, inside-out object, it would probably look like a very strange football. So by no means should you stuff it. Instead, you are about to sew.

## SEWING THE HUMPS

When you last sewed hearts together you sewed around the bottom of the heart, from point A on illustration 40 around to point D.

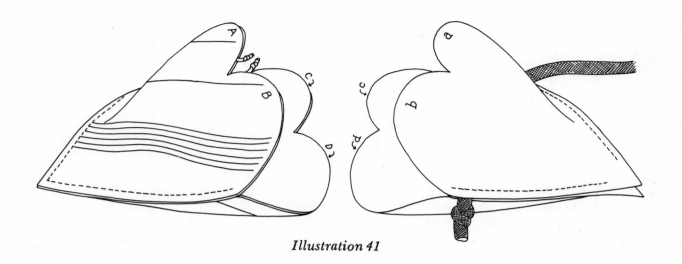

*Illustration 41*

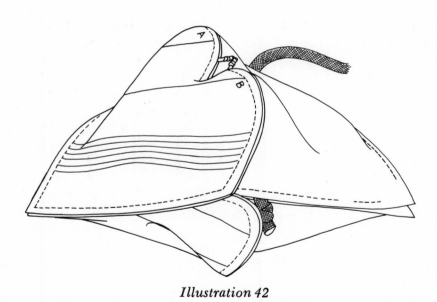

*Illustration 42*

This time, you will still be sewing from point A to point D, but you will be sewing around the top of the heart, over the double hump. Keep in mind that you will have to repeat this procedure twice, and that each time you will be sewing a lining to a quilting, precisely as you pinned it.

### Trimming the curves

Now that all of the machine stitching is done, you must trim the excess seam allowance in order to achieve a really finished look. The top two humps of the heart are the distinguishing shapes that really make a heart look like a heart. But unless they're trimmed properly, they won't look smooth and flowing when the bag is turned right side out. Take a look at illustration 10 on the pear pillow project. You'll note that the curves of the pear are clipped with little inverted points. If you have a good pair of pinking shears, you can cut along the top of the humps and accomplish the same effect as clipping with regular scissors. If you don't, just follow the clipping, as illustrated for the pear, on the curves of your heart.

Cut all four humps in the same manner.

At the bottom tip of the quilted heart, cut off the excess fabric with a straight snip across the point, close to the stitching. (See illustration 43.) Trim evenly along the side of the hearts.

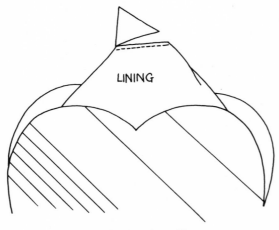

LINING

*Illustration 43*

### Turning your heart right side out

You are about to perform a remarkable magical feat. The strange-looking object you have spent all of this time creating is about to become an elegant evening bag. In fact, the elegant evening bag is hiding inside the strange-looking object—waiting for you to help it out.

There are two points on your object: one at the point of the quilted heart and the other (still unsewn) at the point of your lining heart. Use your hands or whatever probe tool you've been using, and push in the tip of the quilted heart. Keep on pushing, straight down, until you have pushed it through the opening at the bottom of the lining heart. As soon as you see the tip coming through the opening, grab it and pull gently, pushing the fabric back as you pull. You are turning it right side out, exactly as you would the sleeve of a sweater.

When you have most of it turned out properly, put your tool back in the hole and push it along the seam line until you have two attached, recognizable satin hearts.

The bottom of the satin lining heart is still open.

### Sewing the lining closed

The lining heart should be folded inside the quilted heart, but before you put it in place, you need to sew the very bottom of it. Simply pin the two sides of the satin heart together where they're still open, making certain to fold the unfinished edge of the fabric in as you pin. You needn't try to imitate the pointed end of a heart, since the lining won't show, and can instead make a straight line across the bottom of the heart by folding across the point. (See illustration 43.)

Use a small running stitch or a simple overstitch to close the bottom. (See Stitch Glossary.)

Now, with your hand, smooth the lining into the bag.

## REMEMBER THE LOOPS

When you do this final step on the evening

bag, and turn it right side out, you will discover several things that you haven't thought about for a while. First of all, the small loop you inserted at the beginning of the project; the loop will serve as one part of the latch. The second part, the button, will be dealt with in a few minutes.

The second discovery is the strap. Pull on one end of the strap. If it doesn't move, pull the other. One of these ends will be loose, and as you pull, the entire length of the shoulder strap will reveal itself.

With this done, you're ready for the finishing touches.

## BUTTON UP

Jerry was fortunate enough to find a tiny button in the shape of a heart. He was especially fortunate to find the button in red, which matched the red satin of his bag perfectly. But Jerry lives in New York, and fortunately (and unfortunately) you can find *everything* in New York. The particular button you choose will vary from bag to bag, fabric to fabric. The major requirement is that it be tiny and elegant. Look through your old button box if you have one. You might find an antique button in the shape of a flower. I particularly like the idea of a tiny rhinestone button on the black satin. Hold a few different kinds of buttons up to your bag before you actually choose one.

The button, obviously, goes on the side of the bag that doesn't have the loop. To determine button placement, hold the bag closed and pull the loop over the top of the bag to the opposite side. The button should be placed at the bottom reach of the loop, just below the top dip of the heart.

## READY TO GO

Your bag is probably ready to wear now, but it may not all lie as flat as you'd wish. If this is the case you'll have to get out the steam iron and do some pressing, probably along the seams of the heart. Remember, don't put the iron directly on the satin. Use a pressing cloth over your fabric.

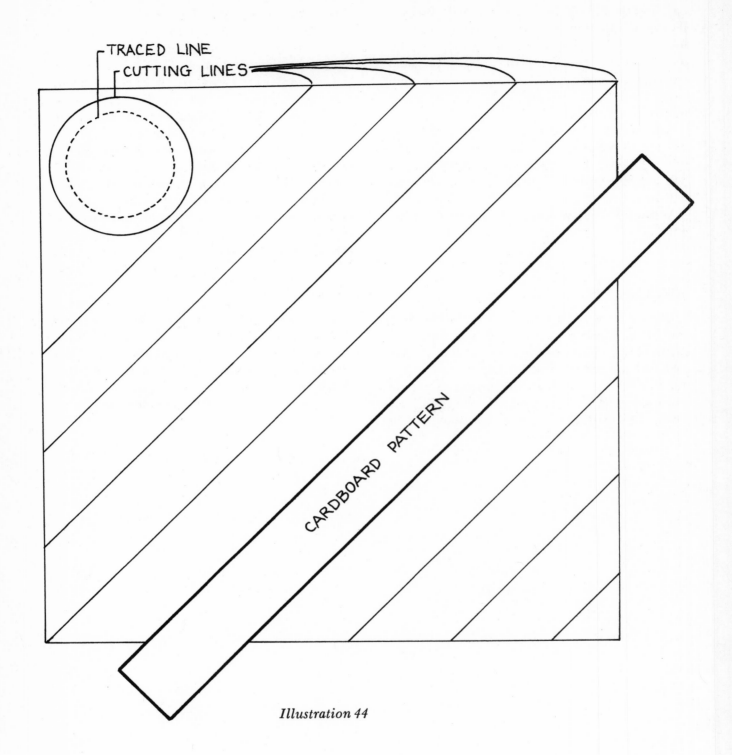

*Illustration 44*

# Coil Pot

The technique of building vessels with coils goes as far back in time as pottery itself. In fact, clay coil building is the predecessor of the potter's wheel. Whatever your involvement with clay has been—whether you've actually taken a course or two in pottery, or just played with your children at the kitchen table—chances are you've made a clay coil. When we were young we used to call the long strings of clay we rolled "spaghetti," and we spent hours rolling long clay spaghettis—often until they broke—and winding coil upon coil into a pot, or a snake, or even a person.

Early in Jerry's work with stuffed fabrics he experimented with fabric coils, and the result of his experimentation is very exciting. He applied the fabric coil to bowls, and to his soft jewelry. The technique he's developed for construction makes the entire process of "soft-coil building" surprisingly easy, and is particularly helpful on the bowl you're about to make. These bowls work well in various sizes and fabrics, and can be hung on a wall in your kitchen. In addition to their being lively-looking, the bowls are functional. Don't, by any means, crack an egg into a fabric bowl, and don't count on service for twelve for soup and sandwiches unless you have a glass bowl that fits inside your fabric one, but there's no reason you can't wash and dry an assortment of fruit and put it out in a fabric bowl. And certainly nonfoods, like spools of thread, or odds and ends that you might keep in a basket, would do just as well in a fabric bowl.

You can make coil bowls in all kinds of fabrics, but they work best with brightly colored cotton. You can use prints and stripes for interesting effects. Since the fabric is cut on the bias, the stripes form a diagonal pattern on the finished bowl. (See color photograph.) The diagonal, wrapped around itself—coil upon coil—works well. But you may want to coordinate your bowl with a particular room. You may have some fabric left over from curtains, or if your bowl will be sitting in the bedroom you can buy an extra pillowcase and match it up with your linen. If you want to make a very formal bowl, you can even use satin. There's virtually no fabric that won't work on this project.

## SPINNING OFF

A bowl is only one of dozens of projects you can make with a coil. The possibilities are infinite. To begin with, you can buy cotton cording in a wide variety of thicknesses. I've recommended a heavy gauge of cording for the bowl because it cuts quantity and construction time in half. Also, I like the way it looks—very soft and stuffed. But you can use thinner cording to make bangle bracelets, chokers, headbands, or belts. Just make shorter coils to fit around whichever part of your body you're making it for, cut, and sew. I'm just a bit over five feet tall, which means that nearly everything I buy to wear requires hemming—which means, of course, that I always have long strips of fabric left over after I hem. These fabric scraps are ideal for making coils.

You can use coils when you make stuffed toys. The biggest-size cotton cording, covered with fabric, would make a dandy snake, and if you combine cording with other types of construction, you can make all kinds of dolls and animals.

Think of all the things that have been made with clay coils. Use the history of coils as a take-off point. Don't let history limit you—let it inspire you!

## WHAT YOU WILL NEED

- 1 yard fabric
- 7″ bowl or flowerpot
- 4½ yards of Number 7 cording
- Elmer's glue  (or equivalent)
- pins
- polyester thread
- cardboard or oak tag

## THE PATTERN

Cut a strip of cardboard 3½″ wide by as long as you can make it. Ideally, it should be long enough to extend beyond the width of your fabric. This strip will serve as your measured ruler when you begin to cut the fabric.

Place the bowl you will be using as your mold on a piece of cardboard, and trace around the outside of the base. When you have drawn the complete circle, cut it out.

## CUTTING THE FABRIC

Lay out your fabric, single layer, on a hard, flat surface. Place the cardboard circle in one corner and trace around it with a felt-tip pen. (If you're using satin, draw the lines with a ball-point pen.) Now lay the strip of cardboard you have just cut along the bias of the fabric. Draw lines tracing both sides of the cardboard strip, and run them off the edge of the fabric as indicated in illustration 44. Pick up the strip, lay it on the line you have just drawn, and continue in that manner until you have drawn diagonals across the entire width of your fabric.

When all of the lines have been drawn, cut out the strips. Then cut out the circle, approximately ½″ outside the line you drew. You needn't be exact about the ½″ margin. Just keep in mind that you will eventually be pasting the fabric over the cardboard, and you'll need enough excess fabric to fold over the edge of the cardboard and glue down.

## SEWING

### Joining the coils

Now that you have done all your cutting, you're ready to join all of the strips of fabric together . . . the first step toward making a long coil.

If you've cut the fabric as indicated in illustration 44, the ends should form angles. Snip off the angles so that your strips are simply long thin rectangles. Lay one strip on top of another, right sides together, wrong sides out, matching up the short end, pin, and sew with ¼″ seam allowance. Repeat this procedure until you have sewn all the long strips together to make one very long strip, approximately five yards long. These short seams should appear as they do in illustration 44. Remember, when you sew the strips together, that you must first place the fabric with the right sides together and the wrong sides facing out in order to create an invisible seam on the right side of the fabric. After you have sewn all the strips together, press the seams open.

When you have made this five-yard-long strip, lay it all out carefully on the floor and fold it lengthwise with the right side of the fabric facing in. (See illustration 45.) Pin carefully along the edge of the long strip and stitch the entire length with ¼″ seam allowance. To insure ¼″ seam allowance, place the outer edge of your machine's presser foot directly on the edge of the fabric. This is a good hint to remember

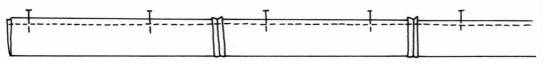

*Illustration 45*

when you want to sew a perfectly straight ¼″ seam.

You should now have a long (approximately five yards) fabric tube. The next step in preparing this tube for its stuffing is to turn it right side out. The process for turning a tube right side out is essentially the same as for turning the sleeve of a sweater right side out. But in the case of *this* tube, it's too long to reach in one end and out the other. So you'll need some help. I suggest the following.

Get as big a safety pin as you can find, and pin it on one end of the fabric. Turn the pin into the tube (see illustration 46) and keep pushing the fabric back on it, until the pin emerges through the other end of the tube you have just sewn. (See illustration 47.)

However you go about it, what you need to do is turn your tube right side out. Perhaps you'll devise your own method for doing this, but the safety-pin process is the best one I've come across.

Now, with your tube turned right side out, you're ready to stuff.

## STUFFING THE COIL

The tube you just made is going to serve as a jacket for the Number 7 cording you bought. To prepare your cording for stuffing, wrap some masking tape around one end. (See illustration 48.) This taping will serve the same function as the little metal tips on the end of your shoelaces. It's pretty hard to thread a shoelace when the tip has come off, and it's equally hard to stuff cotton cording if the end isn't wrapped.

After you have wrapped the end of the cording with tape, stick that big safety pin through it. This time the safety pin is going to serve as your handle. (See illustration 48.)

Insert the pin and the taped end of the cording into one end of the tube you have sewn. Bit by bit, through a process of pulling the pin down through the tube and pulling the tube up over the cording, you will direct the cording through the tube until it's entirely covered.

This procedure will take awhile, but it gets easier as you go along. Just keep in mind what you are trying to accomplish. You have made a

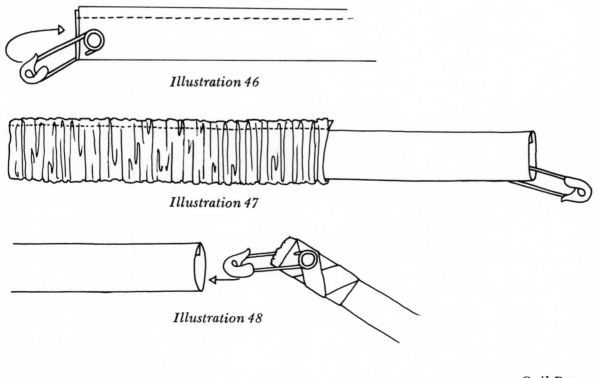

*Illustration 46*

*Illustration 47*

*Illustration 48*

long tube of fabric, which you are going to stuff with cotton cording. It's as simple as that.

Once you have finished stuffing the tube with the cording, your coil is nearly done. To finish it off, simply fold in the raw edge of the fabric on each end of the tube and sew the ends with a simple, small overstitch. (See Stitch Glossary.) With this polishing touch done, your coil is complete, and ready to be formed into a bowl.

## CONSTRUCTING THE BASE

Before you begin to wind the coil you must glue the circle of fabric onto the circle of cardboard. I recommend that you use Elmer's glue for all of your fabric gluing. Spread the glue evenly over the entire surface of one side of the cardboard circle. Make sure to spread the glue evenly. Lay the circle of fabric over the glued circle so that a bit of fabric overlaps evenly around the edge. Now press down on the fabric and hold it for a moment. When you feel it's had a short time to set, turn the circle over and spread glue on the reverse side. Again, make sure you even the glue out smoothly. (Don't worry about your hands. The glue will wash off easily enough.) Fold the overlap of fabric onto this newly glued side of the cardboard and hold it until it sets. Don't worry about how neat this side of the disc is. It won't show when you're finished.

Put this fabric-covered cardboard circle aside for a moment.

## COILING

When I first made a coil pot, I sewed the coils together . . . and the results weren't really very pleasing. The pot didn't look smooth and flowing. The next pot I made I glued together, and the gluing actually worked better than the stitching. But it's a bit tricky to learn. Let me assure you, though, that gluing coil upon coil sounds much more difficult than it actually is, and once you coordinate the hand

with the glue with the hand that's wrapping, this entire project will be a breeze.

So let's begin at the bottom, and work our way up and around.

To make this entire procedure as easy as possible for you to follow, I've arranged the instructions directly under an illustration of each step. Follow the instructions carefully, and keep checking what you're doing against the diagram.

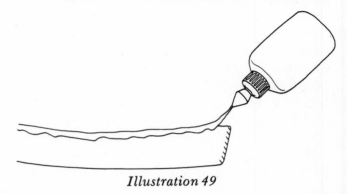

*Illustration 49*

Spread a line of glue along the last foot or so of coil.

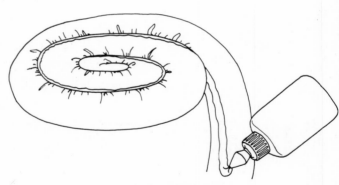

*Illustration 50*

Working on a flat surface, begin winding the coil around itself tightly, so that the glue catches. You must be careful to hold it together tightly as you wrap, or the whole thing will unwind.

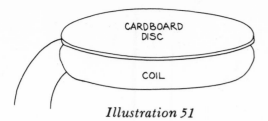

*Illustration 51*

When your wrapped coil is approximately the same size as the cardboard disc, glue the partially covered side of the disc, and spread glue evenly on the flat, coiled surface you have just wrapped. Place the disc over the coil and hold it until it sets. This will be the inside bottom of your bowl.

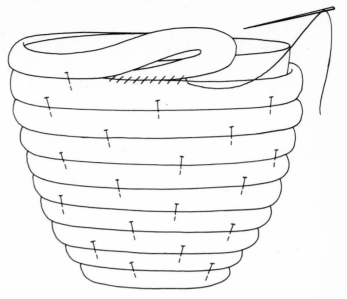

*Illustration 53*

Fold the last 6″ of coil in, as indicated, and sew with a small overstitch (see Stitch Glossary), leaving a bit of coil open for the loop. (This loop is to hang the pot by). Then close the pot by reinforcing it with an overstitch at the point where the end of the coil meets the pot.

**FINAL TOUCHES**

Your coil pot is now finished, but you must be certain that all of the glue is dry. To insure adequate drying time, don't remove the bowl you have wound the fabric around for at least an hour after you've finished gluing. When you do remove it you may find that the pot is stuck to it. Don't be timid. Push down on the top of your fabric pot. It will all squeeze together, like an accordion, and with a bit of pressure it should free itself from the mold.

I'm particularly eager to try a special sculpture that involves two of the projects in this book. I want to make a very big coil pot, perhaps two feet in diameter at the top, and fill it with soft fruit—like the soft pear pillow. It's a bit strange, but I think it will work!

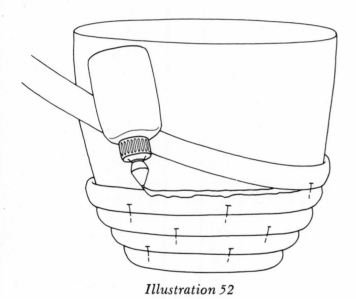

*Illustration 52*

Now place the bowl directly over the base, and slowly wrap your coils around the bowl, gluing as you wrap. You can insert pins as you wrap, to help hold your work together, or you can just hold it with your hands while you work. Continue wrapping and gluing in this manner until you have six inches of coil left. Stop winding, and hold the bowl until dry.

# Sculpted Face Vase

When I first started thinking about doing soft sculpture, I had a very strange dream. In this dream I looked exactly as I normally do, except that I had fabric vines growing from my head instead of hair. All who saw me thought the vines were marvelous, and asked where they might get the same type of thing to replace their own hair.

I'm sure this dream is fraught with all kinds of Freudian significance, but I'll skip over my psyche for the moment and say that I felt very good when I awoke. I felt as if my head was literally sprouting with ideas for soft sculpture; and this face vase was, ironically, one of the ideas I had at the time. I like the vase best when it's holding a live vine. My dream—reversed!

As I said when I introduced the face belt, people have been sculpting faces for as long as people have been sculpting, so the idea of a fabric face is not at all strange. There is, however, a great deal of difference between this vase and the face belt you made earlier.

Throughout the book, the projects have increased in difficulty, but all of them have had very precise instructions. The crucial artistic input in each of the earlier projects has been its design. The construction has been more a matter of developing technique and craft than anything else. In this case, the instructions can't be quite as precise as they have been, since the crucial creative input is as much a part of the construction as it is part of the design. I can't say, "Use one tablespoon of stuffing in the left cheekbone," because the amount of stuffing you use depends on how tightly it's packed, and what look you're after, and other similar variables.

But don't panic! I'm not leaving you entirely on your own . . . yet. The pattern for this vase is traceable, and is very similar to the pattern for the face belt. It's only after you get beyond the initial stages of construction and start to sew the face that you'll have to depend on your artistic eye. It's not at all difficult, and there's a great deal of leeway. You may decide to make your face with a fuller chin, or higher cheekbones, or chubbier cheeks—depending on how much filler you stuff into the fabric for dimension. I'll explain all of this in greater detail when you get to that point of the project, but trust me; this is really lots of fun!

The problem with making a fabric vase is, obviously, that no fabric can hold water. I've gotten around the problem by making this project more of a vase "jacket" than an actual vase. It simply slips over a flowerpot, a glass, or an ordinary vase.

When I began making the project for the first time, I wasn't really sure of what I was doing. I decided early on to make the vase three-sided; one side for the face, and the other two for shape and the hair. I thought perhaps I might paint the face after I had sewn it, and with that in mind, I decided to use a natural-color canvas. As it turned out, I left the face unpainted . . . and I like it that way. The effect is very interesting. People usually see the vase from across the room and assume that it's made from clay.

## SPINNING OFF

As I said earlier, this project differs from the others in that it's more sculpted. And the technique of sculpting loose fibers, as you'll do here, can be applied to any kind of project. You can sculpt animals or toys. The bas-relief that you create on the front of this vase can be used as a wall hanging, sewn onto the back of a denim jacket, or made into a pillow. Whatever you do with the sculpture, it's sure to look interesting.

## WHAT YOU WILL NEED

- 1 yard of off-white cotton canvas
- batting
- dacron stuffing
- typing paper
- carbon paper
- cardboard or oak tag

## MAKING THE PATTERN

Tape together two pieces of typing paper so that they fit over the entire double tracing page (illustration 54), or find a large piece of paper that you can see through. Lay the paper over the tracing page and trace all of the lines of the face, including the outline. Don't be concerned that the tracing page doesn't seem to have as many wrinkles as my vase in the photograph. You'll see, as you sew, that the fabric forms its own lines in response to your stitches.

Place the paper with the pattern over a piece of oak tag and slip some carbon paper, shiny side down, between the two. (One sheet of carbon paper may not be large enough.) Use a ball-point pen to retrace the outline of the face. (See illustration 1.) Set the detailed pattern aside, and cut out the oak tag along the line you have just drawn. Place the oak-tag template aside for later use.

Now lay a new sheet of typing paper over the tracing page that has the nose and the lips (illustration 55) and trace the outline of these features. Remember to trace the nose front and the nose back. When you have duplicated the second tracing page on a sheet of typing paper, lay the typing paper over a piece of oak tag and slip the carbon paper, shiny side down, between the two, just as you did before. (See illustration 1.) Now cut out the templates for the nose and lips and put them aside.

You should now have the following pattern pieces: an oak-tag face template; a detailed paper face pattern; an oak-tag front-nose template; an oak-tag back-nose template; and a lip template.

## CUTTING THE FABRIC

Fold your canvas in half and put a few pins along the edge. Place the oak-tag face template over the fabric on the bias (see illustration 4) and trace around its edge. Lift the template and repeat this procedure two more times, so that you have the outline of three faces drawn on your fabric.

Place the oak-tag lip template on the bias of your doubled fabric and trace around it.

Cut carefully around all the lines you have drawn, and put the fabric faces and lips aside for the moment.

Unfold your leftover fabric and lay it out on a hard, flat surface. Lay the front-nose template and then the back-nose template on the bias of the fabric and trace around the perimeter of each. Remember, you are drawing now on a single layer of fabric. Cut around the lines you have just drawn and set the two pieces of nose aside.

## CUTTING THE BATTING

Lay your batting—double thick—on the floor and place the oak-tag template over it. Hold the template with one hand and cut around the edge. Repeat this process two more times, until you have cut three doubled pieces of batting in the shape of the face.

## TRACING ON THE FACE

Take one of the face-shaped pieces of canvas and lay it flat on a table. Place the detailed paper face pattern over it. Slide a sheet of seamstress tracing paper between the two (see illustration 2), with the colored side down. I recommend that you use yellow paper over the canvas.

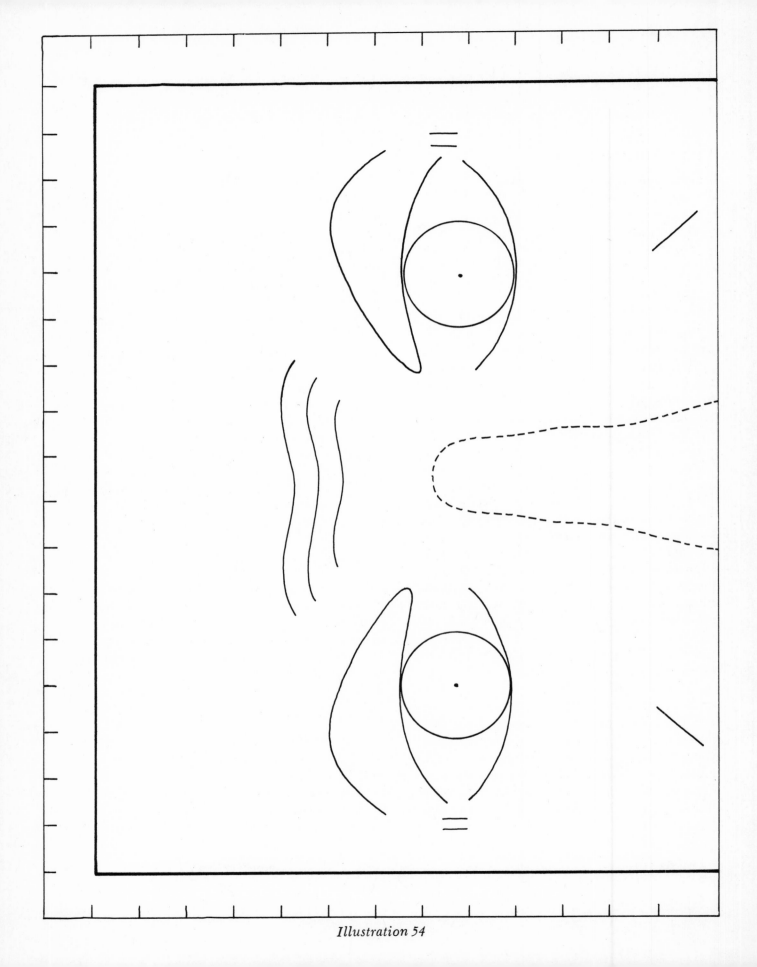

*Illustration 54*

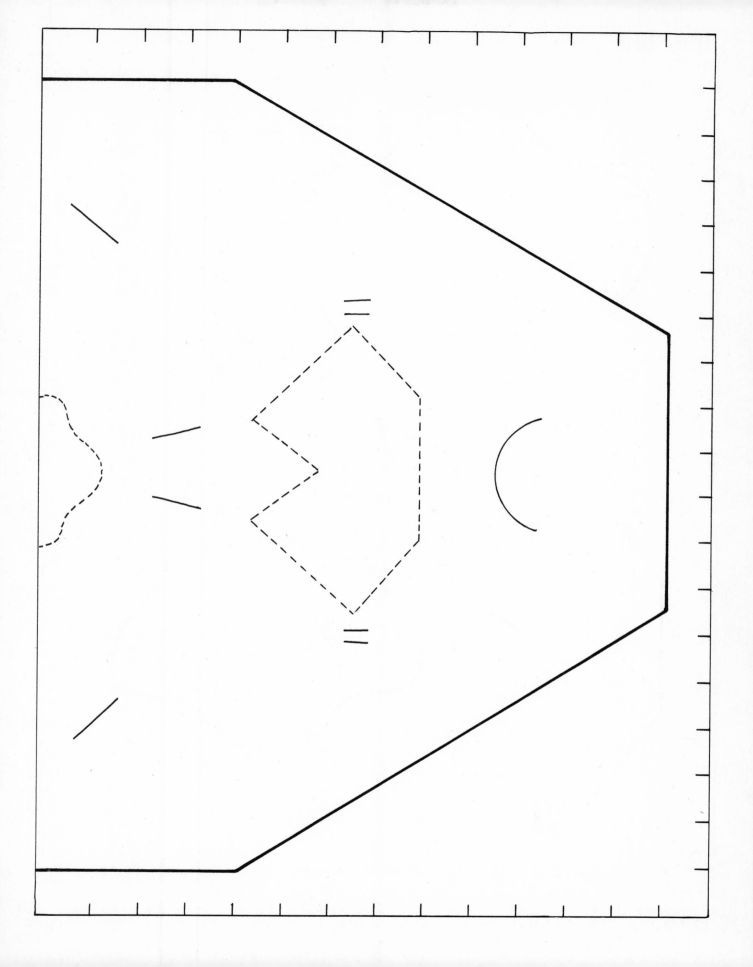

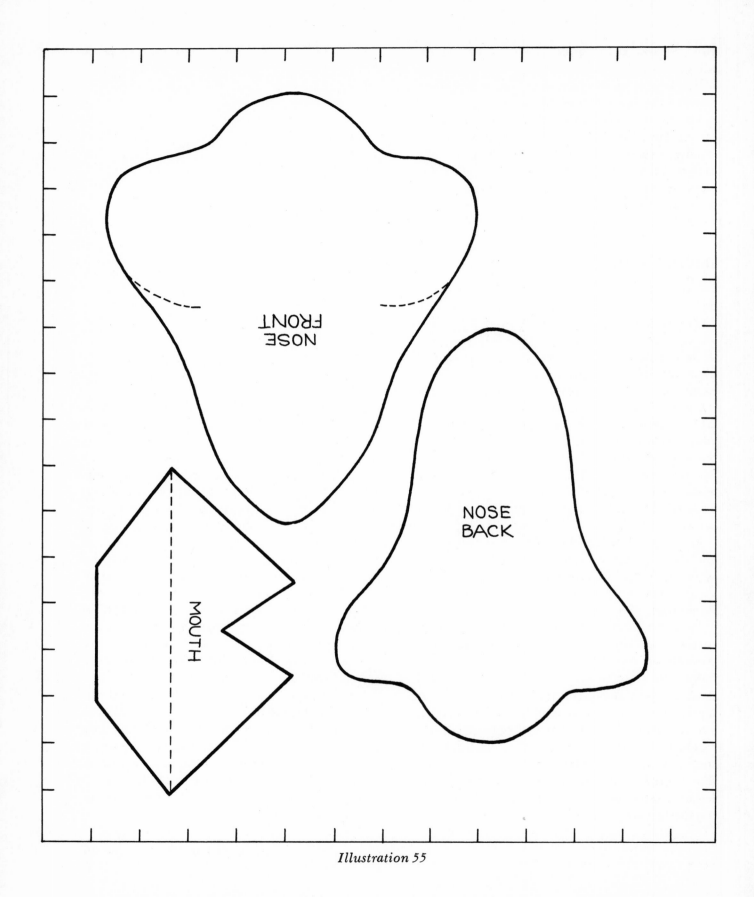

*Illustration 55*

Now retrace all the lines on the paper pattern with a ballpoint pen. The procedure works in the same way as the procedure you followed to transfer the pattern lines to oak tag.

When you have drawn over all of the lines on the face, lift the pattern and the seamstress tracing paper and check the face you have drawn. Then put this piece of canvas aside for a few moments. For the sake of clarity in the next step, let's call this piece of canvas "canvas F."

## SEWING THE FACE SHAPE

Lay a double thickness of face-shaped batting on a table and place canvas F over it, with the yellow lines facing up. These lines will be your sewing guidelines, and they must be facing you if they're to serve any function. Put a second piece of canvas directly over canvas F. (Don't worry about covering the lines. When you turn it right side out, they'll show again.) Pin these layers together around the edge, and put it into your machine with the fabric facing up. Follow the stitching lines of illustration 56, allowing 1/2" for your seam. Make certain to sew *only* where indicated. The gaps in your stitching will be used for stuffing holes when you begin to contour the face.

When you have finished stitching the batting and both pieces of canvas together, trim the seam line down to approximately 1/4" and snip the corners as you did for the heart bag. (See illustration 42.)

With all of this completed, you're ready to turn the face right side out through the opening you left on top. You've done this many times before, so there shouldn't really be a problem this time. Just put your thumbs between the two layers of canvas and turn it inside out. When you're finished, and have poked out the corners carefully, you should have two pieces of canvas stuffed with a double layer of batting. With the face turned right side out, and the lines of the features showing, you're ready to begin attaching the features and sewing.

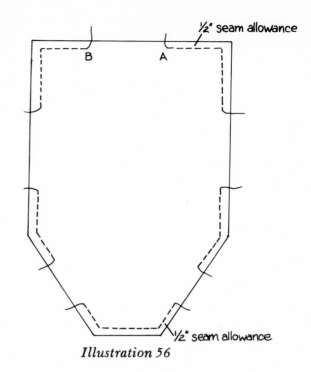

*Illustration 56*

But you still have four other pieces of face-shaped canvas, and two more double layers of face-shaped batting. Lay the double layers of batting next to each other on a table, and put two pieces of the canvas on top of each one. Pin around the edges. Insert one of these pinned pieces into the machine (again, keep the canvas facing up, batting down) and insert the needle on one side of the top opening. Sew around the entire perimeter of the face until you reach the other side of the top opening. Look at illustration 56. You are simply sewing the face to the batting, as you did with canvas F, but instead of leaving all the openings for stuffing, you will sew an unbroken seam from point A around the chin to point B. Repeat this stitching procedure on the third pile of canvas and batting.

When you have sewn around the perimeter of both of the face-shaped pieces, trim the edges as you did earlier, and turn each piece right side out. Since you will not be stuffing or contouring either of these pieces, sew the top openings closed with an overstitch. (See Stitch Glossary.) Make sure to fold the fabric in a bit to conform with the seam line.

## SEWING THE LIPS AND NOSE

### The nose

If you hold the back nose and front nose together you'll see that the front is a bit bigger than the back. This size difference allows for shaping, but complicates sewing. Baste the front- and back-nose pieces together, making certain that the edges are aligned. Don't worry about the excess fabric that gathers in the middle of the nose. So long as the edges are smooth, the rest will straighten out when you stuff it.

After you have basted the nose front to the nose back, insert it into your machine. Follow the stitching lines indicated on illustration 57 and use your presser foot as a guide to insure an even 1/4" seam allowance. Sew very slowly, because the curves around the nostrils are a bit tricky.

When you have finished stitching the nose, notch the curves around the edge, exactly as you notched the curves on other projects (see illustration 10), and turn the nose right side out through the opening at the top.

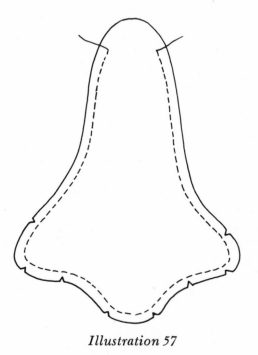

*Illustration 57*

### The lips

Both of the lips are exactly the same size, so you should have no trouble sewing them together. Still, I recommend that you baste before you put them in the machine. Insert the basted lips into the machine and sew, following the stitching lines (illustration 58) on the tracing page. Again, use the presser foot to guarantee an even 1/4" seam allowance. Sew very slowly around the perimeter of the lips, making certain that your corners are sharp. (I recommend the same process for turning corners on this project that you used on the quilted heart bag, page 77). If you followed the stitching lines properly you will have left the bottom seam of the lip open.

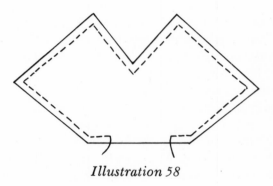

*Illustration 58*

Notch the curves as you did on the nose, and turn the lips right side out. Make sure that all of the points are pushed out and sharp. You may find it helpful to push the back of a paintbrush along the seam lines from the inside, as you did on earlier projects.

## STUFFING THE LIPS AND NOSE

### The nose

Poke little bits of loose stuffing into the nose through the opening at the top, but use a tool to make sure that the stuffing reaches the nostrils. When you attach the nose to the face, you'll be bending the nostrils in, so make certain that you don't overstuff. The nose should be very soft, not stiff and bursting at the seams.

When you have enough stuffing in the nose, fold the edge of the opening in so that it conforms with the seam line (approximately ¼″) and shape the fabric so that the bridge of the nose curves. Stitch it closed with a small overstitch. (See Stitch Glossary.)

When your nose is stuffed and closed, sew a back running stitch as indicated on the nose tracing page to delineate the nostrils. Sew through both layers of fabric and stuffing.

### The lips

Stuff the lips exactly as you did the nose—lightly—but be careful to fill the corners. When they're adequately stuffed, close the bottom opening with a small overstitch, just as you did for the nose.

## SEWING THE FACE

You're ready now to put all of these odd pieces of stuffed fabric together on a face. Find the batted canvas F. With the yellow lines facing you, you're ready to begin attaching features.

### The lips

Place the stuffed lips over the lip lines on the face, and sew them to the canvas with a small overstitch. (See Stitch Glossary.) Try to catch only the first layer of canvas with your needle. When you have sewn around the outline of the lips, knot and break your thread. (See illustration 58.)

On my face, I've sewn a line from one corner of the mouth to the other, separating the upper and lower lips. You may decide that you prefer the more abstract look of the lip without that line of stitching. But if you opt to include the line, just sew it across with a back running stitch, making sure to catch just a bit of stuffing with each stitch.

### The nose

The nose is the most difficult aspect of this project, and it will probably require a bit of work before you're satisfied. The lines for the placement of the nose are indicated on the canvas, just as the lines for the lips are. Start sewing the nose to the canvas at the top, and sew around the top and down to the beginning of each nostril with a small overstitch (see Stitch Glossary), just as you did for the lips. But don't sew across the bottom of the nose. When you get to the beginning of the nostril, fold it in a bit and sew the curve in place. Repeat this same procedure on the other side of the nose. The bottom dip of the nose will be pushed out a bit when the nostrils are sewn, and it should hang down, giving the nose dimension. Look at the photograph of my face to be sure you understand what you're after. With this done, you have completed the most difficult problem in the book!

Since a nose is often what gives a face its character, you may want to do a bit more with the one you've just sewn. Experiment! Hand stitching is easy to rip, so you really have very little to lose. I like what happens when I put a

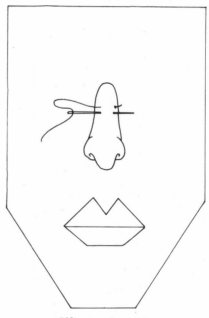

*Illustration 59*

few stitches through the nose (see illustration 59) and pull before I knot. It gathers the fabric together, forming bumps and curves. Try to pull your stitches in different directions. These stitches, and the tension they cause, do wonderful things to a face.

## CONTOURING

By now your face is beginning to look like a face. The nose is on, with its own quirks. The lips are attached, and you're ready to begin shaping. This is where your eye (in fact, this is where both of your eyes) and your judgment really come into play. You will be alternately sewing a line and pushing bits of stuffing against it, through the holes you've left around the perimeter of the face. All of your stuffing should go between the batting and canvas F.

Work slowly on the facial lines and pay close attention to how the fabric responds to your stitching. As you work on the lines I've drawn, you may get some ideas of your own.

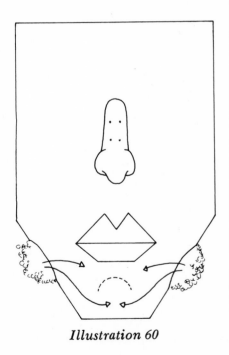

*Illustration 60*

### The chin

Sew over the cleft mark in the chin with a back running stitch. (See Stitch Glossary.) Keep the stitches small, and be sure to sew through all of your fabric. The stitches should be visible on both sides of the canvas. After you have sewn the cleft, push bits of stuffing under, above, and around it, through the openings on either side of the mouth. (See illustration 60.) You should be able to distribute the stuffing in a pleasing way with your fingers, but if by this time you feel more comfortable with the back end of a paintbrush, by all means use that.

When you begin to recognize the shape of a chin, leave it. You won't be closing up the sides of the face until much later and can always come back to add a bit more stuffing.

### The mouth

The mouth is basically finished, but the face needs some lines. Look at yourself in the mirror and smile. You'll probably notice some lines at the corners of your mouth. Whatever your view may be on face lifts and wrinkles, I'm sure that you can recognize how important your lines are in making your face look special and individualized. They're equally important to your soft face.

Sew over the lines on either side of the mouth, but sew only through canvas F. Pull the thread tightly with each stitch, until the fabric puckers and forms a pleat. When you've made a small pleat on each side of the mouth, pull the needle through to the back of the face and knot it.

Next you must sew the two vertical lines between the mouth and the nose. First, sew, with a back running stitch (see Stitch Glossary) along one of the two lines. When you have sewn the line, through both layers of fabric, poke a bit of stuffing against it. (See illustration 61). With the stuffing in place, sew the second line. This second line will serve to lock the stuffing in place.

When you have sewn both vertical lines between the nose and the lips, and locked a bit of stuffing between them, poke more stuffing above and around the lips.

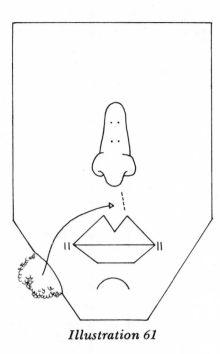

*Illustration 61*

## The eyes

Even with all the contouring you've done on your face until now, it still doesn't look quite as a face should. You'll be startled by the difference two eyes make in a person's appearance. But the eyes are a bit tricky, and to make this important step easier for you, I'm going to give my directions directly under each illustration, as I've done on several other projects. Use a back running stitch on all of this sewing, and run it through both layers of fabric.

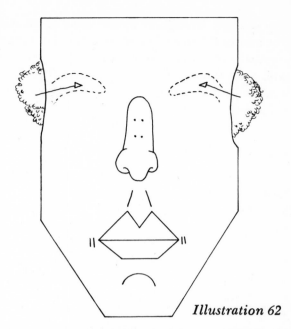

*Illustration 62*

Sew over the lines you've drawn to indicate the eyelid. Poke a bit of stuffing into the space between the two lines.

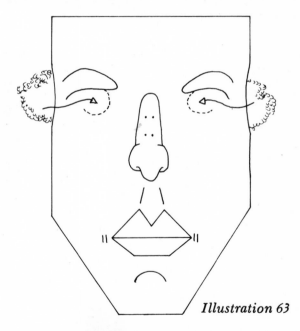

*Illustration 63*

Sew half of the pupil, as indicated, and poke some stuffing into the circle. With this stuffing secured against the curved stitching, finish sewing the circle, thereby locking the tuft of stuffing in place.

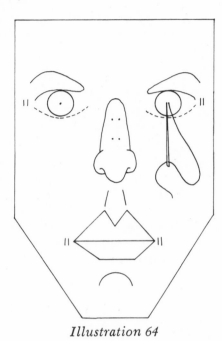

*Illustration 64*

Push your needle and thread from behind through the center of the pupil and make a small, tight stitch, knotting the thread on the back of the face. This stitch gives the eyes some focus—a subtle but important touch. After you have sewn the stitch in the center of the pupil, sew a back running stitch on the bottom line of the eye.

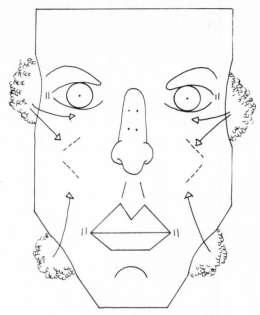

*Illustration 65*

When you have finished sewing the eye, stitch a small pleat at the outer corner of each eye, exactly as you did at each corner of the mouth. Remember, don't sew through all the layers of fabric on the pleat. Just pick up the first layer of canvas—canvas F—with your needle. This pleat will create the illustration of crow's-feet, and add the final touch of life to your eyes.

### Cheekbones

Although you may not succeed in creating a soft Katharine Hepburn, your face is certainly entitled to some contour. And when you talk about facial contour, you're usually talking about cheekbones. Oddly enough, this major aspect of facial contouring can be done with only a few stitches. Again, you'll be sewing with a back running stitch, through all layers of fabric.

Stitch over the lines you've marked on the cheeks. When the stitches are secured firmly, push stuffing against them from either side of the face. (See illustration 65.) The stuffing here can be plentiful, and should really make a marked difference in the appearance of your face. Keep poking the stuffing until the contour is exactly as you want it. Don't worry about overstuffing now, because you can always remove what you've put in.

### *The forehead*

The final touch of life left to be added to your face is a furrowed, wrinkled brow. You don't have to stitch in these wrinkles, but I like them. Simply sew through all layers of fabric, with a back running stitch, over the lines you've drawn on the forehead.

## CLOSING THE FACE

Your face is sewn. Make sure that you're satisfied with the amount of stuffing and with the general appearance of it. When you're happy, you're ready to close up those stuffing holes around the edge. Fold the fabric in, to conform with the seam line, and sew the opening closed with a small overstitch. (See Stitch Glossary.)

## HAIR

You should now have one finished face and two pieces of batted canvas that are shaped like the face. Before you sew these three parts of the vase together, you'll want to add the suggestion of hair. (Keep in mind that you're not required to add hair. If you like the way things look just as they are, skip this step entirely.) There are a vast number of ways you can go about adding hair to your face. You can loop it, as you did on the face belt (see Stitch Glossary), or you can hand stitch long strands of wool. But I sewed my hair on by machine, the simplest solution to a very simple problem.

If your machine has a zigzag stitch, you can use it for the hair; if not, I suggest a large machine-basting stitch. If your machine does all sorts of fancy embroidery, your options are far greater than mine were.

Insert canvas F into the machine, face up, and run your machine stitching all over the forehead, keeping the lines basically vertical.

(See illustration 66.) Repeat this procedure on the other two pieces of canvas, but this time run your stitches down the entire length of the fabric. Stop whenever you think there's enough hair. (See illustration 67.)

You may decide to use a contrasting-color thread on the hair. I've found that yellow thread works very well. It's not too sharp a contrast, but it is a bit of variation.

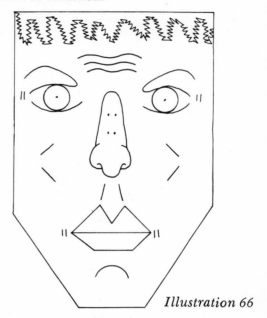

*Illustration 66*

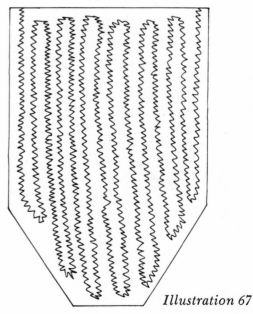

*Illustration 67*

## SEWING THE VASE TOGETHER

Your vase is nearly done. The last step is to put it all together . . . a very easy task. Simply thread a needle, and double your thread. Hold canvas F next to one of the other pieces of batted canvas and align the sides so that the tops meet. Sew the sides together, from the outside, with a small overstitch. Keep the stitches small, so that they don't show, but pull the thread firmly. If you have button thread, use that. It's stronger than ordinary thread.

Sew the second piece of canvas to the other side of canvas F, and then sew the two faceless pieces of canvas together.

When you've finished sewing the three-sided vase together, find a glass that fits nicely inside it, then go out and buy some fresh flowers to fill it!

# *Stitch Glossary*

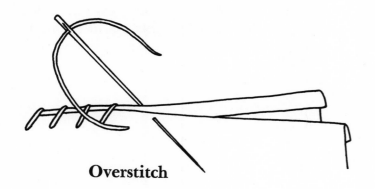

**Overstitch**

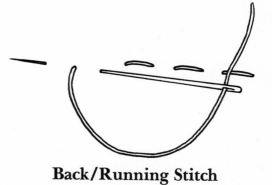

**Back/Running Stitch**

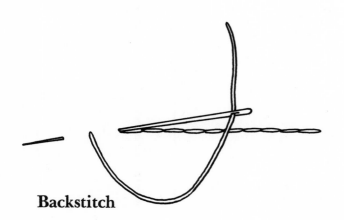

**Backstitch**

**Looping Wool for Hair on Face Belt**

**Basting/Running Stitch**

# Index

poster board, 36
pot, fabric coil, **88,** 89–93, **90–93**
projects, 31–106
   photographs, 10
   skills, 7
   spinoffs, 10

Qiana, 15
quilting, 10, 80–82, **80–82**

rags, 21, 24
rainbow necklace, 49–53, **50, 52**
rayon, 12
reducing designs, 31, 36
ribbons, 27
rubber, foam, 21, 23–24
running stitch, **107**

sand, 21, 25
satin, 12, 14–15, 63, 69, 77, 79, 89
satin stitch, 65
satin weave, 13
sawdust, 21, 24–25
Scovill Dritz Tracing Paper, 8
sculpted face vase, 94–106, **96–105**
sheet foam, 21, 23–24
shoulder strap, bag, **83,** 84
shredded foam, 21, 23–24
silk, 12
silk screen, 10
single knits, 13, 16
skills, project, 7
snake, stuffed, 89
snaps, 27
stitch glossary, 10, **107**
strawberry pillow, 35

stuffing
   fabric compatibility, 22
   material, 7, 21–25
   process, 34, 39–40, 91–92, **91,** 100–101
sun necklace, 49
synthetic fibers, 12, 14, 21, 22–23

tabby weave, 12
terry cloth, 15
texture, fabric, 14, 15, 16
top stitching, 41, 73–74, **74**
toys, stuffed, 89, 94
tracing pages, 8–9, **30, 37, 44, 45, 50, 56, 57, 62, 78, 88, 96–98**
tracing paper, 8, **8**
trimmings, 27, 54
twill weave, 13

vase, sculpted face, 94–106, **96–105**
Velcro, 27
velour, 15, 16, 77
velvet, 15, 16
velveteen, 16
voile, 14

wall hangings
   auto, 54
   cloud, 49
   face, 95
   pin, 31
washing, 12, 14, 16, 17, 22, 23, 24
weaves, 12–13
wool, 12, 18, 67, 105
workability, fabric, 14, 15, 16, 17, 18
woven fabrics, 14–16

zigzag stitch, 58, 105
zippers, 27